3

A Rose
For Every Purpose

A simple collection of English roses and old garden roses (below) illustrates the ease of blending color and form into a masterpiece for the indoors: 'Golden Celebration' (cupped yellow), 'Evelyn' (flat, creamy white), 'Baronne Prevost' (quartered, medium pink), and 'Salet' (light pink).

By any other name, of course, this blossom would smell as sweet. But no matter what the century or culture, people have always celebrated the rose. From ancient times to today, in poetry and song, during wars and festivities, people from all walks of life have honored this "Queen of Flowers." In fact, in recognition of the rich history and versatility of this beloved blossom and our long-standing relationship with it, the United States Congress has selected the rose as this country's national flower. Roses are available in so many shapes, sizes, colors, and fragrances that almost every garden has a place for at least one, proving that successful rose growing is within everyone's reach.

Because roses are available in so many forms, few plants can rival their benefit in the home landscape. From the sweetest miniature rose potted in a container to the most profuse rambler cascading along a fence, from the fragrant charm of an old-fashioned garden rose to the stately elegance of a hybrid tea, there is a rose to suit every garden and gardener.

Roses provide structure and proportion to the landscape. They come in every shape, size, and color imaginable. And with today's long-lasting repeat bloomers, roses are among the most showy and hardworking of all garden plants. Regardless of your tastes or gardening style—whether it's casual and relaxed or tailored and formal—roses can be a welcome addition to your living environment.

INDOOR-OUTDOOR APPEAL

Fresh-cut roses from the garden brought into the house are a lovely reward. Filling up a vase with roses is easy, and the results are spectacular. A collection of pastel English roses and perfumed old garden roses can create a wonderfully serene arrangement. Bright colors add vibrancy to a room. And sweet-scented blooms are, of course, an added bonus.

Many serious rose growers are eager to experiment with new varieties as they appear

Formal rose gardens (right) employ low-growing hedges like boxwood to define precise boundaries.

ORTHO'S All About
Roses

Written by Dr. Tommy Cairns

Meredith₀ Books
Des Moines, Iowa

Ortho® Books
An imprint of Meredith® Books

Ortho's All About Roses
Editor: Michael McKinley
Art Director: Tom Wegner
Copy Chief: Catherine Hamrick
Copy and Production Editor: Terri Fredrickson
Contributing Editor: James A. Baggett,
  Leona Holdsworth Openshaw
Technical Consultants: Anne Graber, Clair G. Martin III,
  Edward J. Pagliai, Delores K. Pagliai
Contributing Writer: Martin Miller
Contributing Copy Editor: Chardel Gibson Blaine
Contributing Proofreaders: Kathy Eastman, Steve Hallam,
  Sheila Mauck, JoEllyn Witke
Technical Research Assistant: Carolyn S. Magnani
Contributing Illustrators: Mavis Torke, Pam Wattenmaker,
  Cyndie Wooley
Contributing Prop/Photo Stylist: Alice Hart
Indexer: Donald Glassman
Electronic Production Coordinator: Paula Forest
Editorial and Design Assistants: Kathleen Stevens,
  Karen Schirm
Production Director: Douglas M. Johnston
Production Manager: Pam Kvitne
Assistant Prepress Manager: Marjorie J. Schenkelberg

Additional Editorial Contributions from
  Art Rep Services
Director: Chip Nadeau
Designers: Teresa Marone, Laura Rades
Illustrators: Glory Bechtold, Shawn Wallace

Meredith® Books
Editor in Chief: James D. Blume
Design Director: Matt Strelecki
Managing Editor: Gregory H. Kayko
Executive Ortho Editor: Benjamin W. Allen

Director, Sales & Marketing, Retail: Michael A. Peterson
Director, Sales & Marketing, Special Markets:
  Rita McMullen
Director, Sales & Marketing, Home & Garden Center
  Channel: Ray Wolf
Director, Operations: George A. Susral

Vice President, General Manager: Jamie L. Martin

Meredith Publishing Group
President, Publishing Group: Christopher M. Little
Vice President, Consumer Marketing & Development:
  Hal Oringer

Meredith Corporation
Chairman and Chief Executive Officer: William T. Kerr
Chairman of the Executive Committee: E.T. Meredith III

On the cover: The award-winning hybrid tea rose
'Signature'. Photograph by Kathy Longinaker

All of us at Ortho® Books are dedicated to providing you
with the information and ideas you need to enhance your
home and garden. We welcome your comments and
suggestions about this book. Write to us at:
  Meredith Corporation
  Ortho Books
  1716 Locust St.
  Des Moines, IA 50309–3023

Thanks to
Luis Desamero, Melissa George, Colleen Johnson, Aimee
  Reiman, Mary Irene Swarz
Photographers
(Photographers credited may retain copyright ©
  to the listed photographs.)
L= Left, R= Right, C= Center, B= Bottom, T= Top
William D. Adams: 59TR; American Rose Society: 92; Arena Rose
Co.: 82BL, 85CL, 86BR; Richard Baer: 57BR, 58CR, 59CL, 59BC,
65TR, 68TL, 69TL, 69 Row 3-1, 68TL, 70TC, 70 Row 2-3, 70BL, 71
Row 3-2; M. Baker: 11R; Laurie Black: 58BR; T. Cairns/Studio City:
24-25T, 54BR, 69TC, 70 Row 3-1; David Cavagnaro: 72BL, 72BR,
73BR, 80BL inset, 81 Row 2-1, 89BR; Crandall & Crandall: 55TL,
56BC, 65BC; R. Todd Davis: 60C, 67BL, 80BL; Alan & Linda Detrick:
56TC, 60TR, 61CR, 69TR, 74TC, 79TR; John E. Elsley: 55CR, 57BL,
61CL, 61BL, 62BL, 63TC, 64TC, 65TL, 65C, 65CR, 66TR, 66C, 67TC,
67TR, 67BC, 73TL, 73CR, 73BC, 74TL, 76TC, 76C, 78TL, 79TL, 79
Row 3-3, 80TC, 80TR, 80 Row 2-2, 80BC, 80BR, 81TL, 81 Row 3-3,
81BL, 82TL, 82BR, 83TC, 83TR,83CL, 83C, 83CR, 83BL, 84TR, 84
Row 2-3, 84 Row 3-2, 84BL, 84BR, 85TL, 85TR, 85CR, 85BL, 85BC,
86TL, 86TR, 86CL, 86C, 86CR, 86BL, 87TL, 87TR, 87CL, 87CR, 87BL,
87BR, 89TL inset, 89 Row 4-2, 90TL, 90 Row 2-2, 91TL, 91TC, 91TR,
91 Row 2-1 & 2; Derek Fell: 14TL, 54TL, 54BL, 55TC, 56BL, 57TL,
60TL, 63C, 64BR, 66TL, 67BR, 79 Row 3-1, 80TL, 80 Row 3-1, 89TL,
89TR, 90 Row 3-1, 90BR; John Glover: 4BR, 14TC, 16BL, 16BC, 16BR
(David Stevens), 20BR, 66BR, 72TL, 73TR, 74CR, 75BR, 77BL, 78TR,
78BR, 79BR, 84 Row 3-1, 85TC, 86BC, 88TL, 90 Row 3-2; David
Goldberg: 12BL, 15BR, 19BR, 80 Row 3-1; Goodman: 91 Row 4-1 & 2;
Mick Hales: 10B; Jerry Harpur: 12TL, 12BR, 13BR, 14TR, 16TR,
17TC, 20BL, 21BR, 22T, 22C, 83TL; Lynne Harrison: 9B, 17CR, 75TR,
85BR, 90BL; Horticultural Photography: 63BL, 73BL; Jackson &
Perkins: 91 Row 3-1, 91BL, 91BR; Dency Kane: 79 Row 3-2 inset,
81BR, 89CR; Michael Landis: 21BL; Andrew Lawson: 74BR, 75BL
inset, 80 Row 3-2, 81 Row 2-3, 85C; Kathy Longinaker: 4BL, 8, 9TR,
9CR, 14B, 18BL, 25B, 30BL, 30-31, 31 all, 44, 45 all, 59BR, 60CR,
60BR, 61BL, 63CL, 64CR, 65TC, 65BR, 68TR, 69BR, 70TR, 71 Row 2-
2, 71BR, 75CL inset, 76BL, 76BR, 77TC, 79 Row 2-1, 81 Row 2-2,
84TL, 84 Row 3-3, 86TC, 88BR; Janet Loughrey: 5, 62TL, 66TC, 66BL,
66BC, 67C, 71TR, 71 Row 3-3, 74CL, 75TC, 81TR; Charles Mann:
13TR; David McDonald/PhotoGarden: 5 inset, 15TR, 17BC, 56BR,
58TR, 58BL, 59TL, 63TR, 63BR, 64TL, 64BL, 64BC, 65BL, 68BL,
69 Row 2-3, 69 Row 3-2, 70 Row 2-2, 70BR, 73TC, 73CL, 74C, 74BL,
74BC, 75TL, 77BR, 80 Row 2-3, 81TC, 81 Row 3-2 inset, 82TR, 84 Row
2-1, 88TR & inset, 89 Row 2-1 & 2, 89BL, 89BR inset, 90 Row 2-1,
90BC; Clive Nichols: 16TL (Wollerton Old Hall, Shropshire), 17BR
Meadows Plants, Berkshire), 19TL (Cherries Manor, Buckinghamshire);
E.J. Pagliai: 70 Row 3-2; Jerry Pavia: 17TL, 22B, 57BC, 58TL, 59CR,
62TR, 62BR, 64CL, 64C, 66CR, 75CL; Joanne Pavia: 57CL, 59BL; Ben
Phillips/Positive Images: 79TR inset; Cheryl R. Richter: 19C; Field
Roebuck: 15CL, 19BC, 91 Row 3-3; Susan A. Roth: 17TR, 17CL, 17C,
54TR, 56TL, 64TR, 67CL, 70 Row 2-1, 75CR, 75BL, 78BL, 79TC, 84
Row 2-2, 89TR inset; Gene Sasse: 63TL; Ron Shaw: 55CL, 55BL,
56TR, 57TR, 60CL, 60BL; Richard Shiell: 15BL, 23, 55TR, 55BR,
57CR, 58TC, 58CL, 61TR, 63CR, 63BC, 65CL, 67TL, 67CR, 68BR,
69 Row 2-1, 69 Row 2-2, 69BL, 70TL, 71TL, 71 Row 2-1, 71 Row 3-1,
71BL, 71BC, 72TR, 74TR, 76TL, 76TR, 76CL, 76CR, 77TR, 77C,
77CR, 79 Row 3-4, 79BC, 80 Row 2-1, 81 Row 3-4, 81BR inset, 83BR,
87C; Pam Spaulding/Positive Images: 77BC; Albert Squillace/Positive
Images: 61BC, 77TL, 77CL, 88BL; Michael S. Thompson: 17BL, 20BC,
61TL, 66CL, 79 Row 2-2, 79BL, 84TC, 89CL, 91 Row 3-2; J.A.
Wilkinson/VALAN PHOTOS: 38, 39

Note to the Readers: Due to differing conditions, tools,
and individual skills, Meredith Corporation assumes no
responsibility for any damages, injuries suffered, or losses
incurred as a result of following the information published
in this book. Before beginning any project, review the
instructions carefully, and if any doubts or questions remain,
consult local experts or authorities. Because codes and
regulations vary greatly, you always should check with
authorities to ensure that your project complies with all
applicable local codes and regulations. Always read and
observe all of the safety precautions provided by
manufacturers of any tools, equipment, or supplies,
and follow all accepted safety procedures.

Ortho® is a trademark of Monsanto Company used
under license.

in the marketplace. Dedicated hobbyists use this knowledge to improve their rose gardens. Their enthusiasm can be contagious, and casual gardeners can translate that experience into their own gardens. Even if the novice has limited space, a flush of antique roses scrambling over a fence, wall, or trellis is a breathtaking sight. Even a few miniature roses spilling from pots on a terrace are a charming addition of color and dimension.

There's no limit to the number of ways to use roses. In the pages that follow, you will discover practical suggestions for incorporating roses into your landscape. You will also find easy, step-by-step growing instructions, plus a gallery of more than 350 recommended varieties. The most popular of all flowers is unfortunately often misused and misunderstood. Choosing the right roses is half the battle; the other is caring for them intelligently. Take advantage of the versatility of roses, and you will enjoy their delightful gifts for years to come.

An informal rose garden (left) can be a clever blend of roses and companion plants to create a tapestry of color. The simple abundance of the shrub 'Lavender Lassie' gently covering an archway adds romance and provides a central focus, even in a small garden (above).

Knowing the Forms

When selecting roses for your garden, the architectural shape and ultimate dimensions are important. They give form to the landscape and proportion to its elements. Fortunately, you can grow roses almost anywhere that gets six hours of sun a day. Grow them as flowering shrubs, in mixed beds and borders, among herbs in containers, underplanted with annuals, surrounding a mailbox or lightpost, screening a fence, scrambling up trees, trailing over arches or arbors, and cascading down a bank or over a stone wall. The key is to ensure that the variety or varieties you choose are suitable for the use you have in mind.

Environmental factors and personal preference aren't the only considerations that influence the selection process. How a rose is used in the landscape—as an accent, a hedge, or a backdrop in a border—also determines which one is best. If you intend to train the rose up a wall or along a fence, for example, then climbing roses or ramblers are best. For a mass planting, hybrid teas and grandifloras may be dramatic, but they don't work well by themselves as single specimens. The flowers are quite spectacular, but their sometimes leggy form can be unattractive. A shrubbier rose might be a better choice as a single plant in the existing landscape. Shrub roses have a rounded form that works as a blooming hedge as well.

If your garden provides the necessary sunlight and soil conditions—and if you take a little time to explore your home landscape—you can pick the rose that's right for you. Use the helpful illustrations and brief descriptions on these pages to explore the various roses that will thrive in your own backyard.

A. PATIO TREE:
A wonderful way to grow floribundas and miniatures about 4 feet off the ground. Excellent for containers. Exposed plants may be susceptible to winter damage.

B. MINIATURE:
Dense, low-growing roses that cover themselves with tiny blooms, usually in clusters. Use for edging, growing in pots or rockeries, or as a pot plant indoors. Reaches 18 to 24 inches high.

C. FLORIBUNDA:
Known for its large clusters of medium-sized blooms that cover the bush all season long. Generally hardy and easy to care for. Usually grows to about 3 feet high.

D. HYBRID TEA:
The cut flower *par excellence*, easily recognized for the single, sculptural, high-centered bloom per long stem. The florets are usually large and symmetrical. Can reach up to about 5 feet high.

E. CLIMBER:
Actually a shrub with long, arching stems, these roses grow 6 to 20 feet high when trained on walls, trellises, and fences. Train the long canes in a horizontal position to promote bloom production.

F. PILLAR:
A smaller category of climbing roses, this type is often trained around a tall vertical support, covering itself with flowers at each lateral. Can reach heights between 6 to 10 feet tall.

G. OLD GARDEN ROSES:
(Types of roses that existed before 1867.) Wide range in size, shape of bush, and flower form. Can grow 6 to 8 feet high or more. Many bloom only once. Often fragrant.

H. GRANDIFLORA:
Similar to hybrid teas, but identified by their unique ability to send up clusters of large hybrid tea-type blossoms on strong straight stems. Plants are normally 6 to 8 feet tall.

I. MODERN SHRUB:
Recent hybridizing breakthroughs that combine old garden rose flower form and fragrance with modern colors and recurrent blooms. Plants are 6 to 7 feet high.

J. GROUND COVER:
A landscaping category of vigorous, disease-resistant, low-growing plants that spread up to 8 feet wide for bedding and massing. Varieties are usually hardy.

K. STANDARD TREE ROSE:
Excellent choice to grow hybrid teas and floribundas about 6 feet off the ground, often for formal effects. Subject to winter damage in northern areas if left unprotected.

L. RAMBLER:
Given adequate space, this type of rose will grow 30 feet in every direction to cover a tree or even a house. Generally winter hardy. Often has only one bloom cycle each year.

Flowers, Fruit, and Foliage

Roses offer close-inspection beauty of astonishing variety.

EVERY KIND OF FLOWER

All roses are not created equal: There is great variation in number of petals, color combinations, size and shape of the blossoms, as well as their fragrances.

The number of petals is a measure of the fullness of a flower. Roses range from the simplest five-petaled blossom to the fullest flowers of 100 petals or more. Petals, in turn, have their own structure, whether it is plain, reflexed, ruffled, or frilled like a carnation. Flower colors offer a wide selection—single, bi-color, multi-color, blended, striped, and "handpainted." The overall shape of the blossom comes in an equally diverse selection—globular, open-cupped, quartered, flat, rosette, pompon, and high-centered (often called exhibition form).

Another criterion for selecting roses is referred to as "substance of the petals," which measures the durability of the petals. Petals with substance are tougher. They feel thicker than more delicate petals—almost leathery. These blossoms last longer and can better sustain exposure to high temperatures.

THE BONUS OF ROSE HIPS

Some roses that produce only one bloom cycle in the spring have the added value of putting on an autumn display of attractive fruit (called "hips"). Most shrub roses and old garden roses are especially good for hips. They produce that extra bonus of massive clusters of rose hips of various shapes and sizes—round, elongated, even prickly. For instance,

'Signature'
High centered
Hybrid tea

'Playboy'
Single
Floribunda

'Golden Celebration'
Cupped
Modern shrub

'Blueberry Hill'
Semidouble
Floribunda

'Evelyn'
Flat open
Modern shrub

'Salet'
Quartered pompon
Old garden rose

'Madame Hardy'
Quartered with
central pip
Old garden rose

'Aunt Gerry'
Fully opened
Hybrid tea

'Frau Dagmar Hartopp' has some of the largest tomato-like red hips. An interesting display of hips extends the pleasure of roses well into fall and winter.

DON'T FORGET THE FOLIAGE

Rose foliage is an often overlooked yet important ornamental feature, as it appears long before the first blossom and remains prominent throughout the growing season. Leaves can be glossy, semi-glossy, or matte in a range of colors from light green to dark green, even bronze-tinted and gray-green. All these factors contribute to a versatile plant with outstanding traits. In general, glossy foliage is more resistant to fungal attack such as powdery mildew because the waxy coating provides a barrier to the disease.

Single-petaled roses have 5 to 12 petals; 5 is the most common. These roses reflect the charm, elegance, and simplicity of their early ancestors. Shown here is the classic rugosa variety, 'Frau Dagmar Hartopp'.

THE MOST FRAGRANT ROSES

HYBRID TEAS
'Double Delight'
'Fragrant Cloud'
'Keepsake'
'Mister Lincoln'
'Paradise'
'Royal Highness'
'Sheer Bliss'

FLORIBUNDAS
'Angel Face'
'Apricot Nectar'
'Iceberg'
'Margaret Merrill'
'Scentimental'
'Sheila's Perfume'
'Shocking Blue'
'Sunsprite'

MINIATURES
'Rainbow's End'
'Scentsational'
'Sweet Chariot'
'Tropical Twist'

OLD GARDEN ROSES
'Autumn Damask'
'Apothecary's Rose'
'Ispahan'
'Sombreuil'
'Souvenir de la Malmaison'
'Zephirine Drouhin'

SHRUBS
'Fair Bianca'
'L.D. Braithwaite'
'Othello'
'Perdita'
'Constance Spry'
'Guy de Maupassant'
'Johann Strauss'
'Martine Guillot'
'Radio Times'
'The Prince'
'Tamora'

Semi-double roses have 12 to 16 petals, usually forming two or three rows of petals with the fully open blossom showing off the yellow central stamens. This is the floribunda 'Blueberry Hill'.

BEST VARIETIES FOR HIPS

Hips come in a wide variety of shapes and colors. Generally, the largest display of hips come from old garden roses:
'Dortmund'
'Kathleen'
'Frau Dagmar Hartopp'
Rosa rugosa rubra
'Altissimo'

By definition, a double rose has 17 to 25 petals, a full rose has 26 to 40 petals, and a very full rose boasts 41 or more. The blossom has elegance, symmetry, and diversity of form. Shown here, the old garden rose 'Cardinal de Richelieu' bears 40 to 50 petals.

Integrating Roses into the Landscape

The lush flowers and bushy habit of 'Betty Prior' create a lovely poolside hedge. A dependable summer-long bloomer, it is one of the best floribunda roses for the landscape.

A Rose for Every Situation

Because of their dynamic range in color, size, shape, and growth habit, roses lend themselves to a variety of garden situations. Before choosing varieties for your garden, take a moment to evaluate your landscaping requirements. These simple guidelines will help you decide the where and how:

■ Decide on the role you want the rose to perform in the space you have allotted, whether it is for cutting for the home, showy borders, impenetrable hedges, privacy fences, walls, trellises, spots of color in containers on a terrace, or fragrance near the patio.

■ Start small and allow for later expansion as you experience success and satisfaction. But beware of the "Vanishing Lawn Syndrome"—

your devotion to roses may increase to an addiction, as you slowly carve out more space!

■ Select a garden style that pleases you, from the casual country-cottage look to the most formal. Keep in mind the surrounding plants and landscape as you make these decisions.

■ Decide on an exact location—whether it fits into an existing garden or a whole new concept in the landscape. Make sure the location can support your dream roses with plenty of sunshine (at least six hours daily), fertile soil, and adequate drainage.

■ Develop a simple plan and allow the practice of garden-making to inspire your evolving tastes and needs. Sketch out your ideas on paper and try to estimate costs.

■ Finally, peruse the "Rose Selection Guide" starting on page 50 to find the rose that's sure to succeed within your specific requirements.

ADD A SENSE OF DRAMA

A classic method for employing roses in the home landscape is to create living barriers or walls of color. For instance, dress up that streetside fence with a stunning hedge of roses in front—floribundas, low ground covers, or even a low-growing climber or shrub trained

Bouquets of red roses spill over a classic rail fence, creating a classic cottage look (below). Roses can be the perfect low-maintenance plants for adding color to your yard. Imagine this landscape without roses on the fence. Your landscape will look better if you match the type of rose you plant to the style of fence it's on. For eye-popping color and hardiness, it's hard to beat this border of pink 'Winifred Coulter' floribunda roses (right).

along the rails. Multiple plants of a single variety can provide a pleasing unified and rewarding effect. Include fragrance in your hedge as an extra gift to passersby. Try one of the Simplicity series that comes in white, red, purple, pink, and yellow, or the neon-orange floribunda, 'Livin' Easy'.

Add a finishing touch to perennial beds with a border of white miniatures or low-growing floribundas in front—or use them to adorn a pathway leading to the front door, a bed along the drive, or in masses around each side of your patio. An excellent choice would be the popular white floribunda, 'Iceberg', or the white miniature rose, 'Gourmet Popcorn'.

Create a solid bank of color with roses on a hillside or steep slope that's much easier to maintain than lawn grass. Some ground cover roses are ideal for this purpose—for instance, any of the Flower Carpet series.

If your purpose for growing roses is to provide cut flowers for your home, concentrate on varieties with strong straight stems and fragrant blossoms. Site them where harvesting will not disrupt your colorful garden display. Choose from elegantly sculptured flowers of hybrid teas, or the wide color range and informal flower forms provided by modern shrub roses.

Climbing roses do not attach themselves, but must be tied to a support, such as a trellis (above, 'Maigold') or a pergola (right, 'Sally Holmes'). Climbing roses come in all classes and flower forms.

What better way to employ the vigorous and popular climbing rose 'Zephirine Drouhin' than training it to scramble up the side of a house (far right).

Climbers and Ramblers

Perhaps the most dramatic way to use roses in the landscape is to employ climbers, pillars, and standards. They elevate blossoms to eye level and higher, creating a vertical display that most perennials and annuals just can't compete with. It is a romantic vision that adds accent and beauty to any garden. There are many ways to incorporate climbers into the garden, including fences, walls, trellises, arbors, pergolas, and gazebos. If you have the space, you can even grow roses up the trunk of a tree.

FOR FENCES AND WALLS

Consider converting that weather-beaten split-rail fence (or even an unsightly chain-link fence) into a curtain of color. Lush foliage can fill in the spaces, adding both a sense of depth and separation. The long canes produced by climbing varieties can be woven neatly in and out of the structure as they grow. Plant one variety at regular 4 to 5 foot intervals and the intertwining canes will eventually produce a solid wall of beauty and fragrance. Normal grooming and training over several years will create a charming tapestry.

In order to cover a wall in the garden, train the canes into position using supports. On masonry walls, a series of eye bolts with wires arranged horizontally or in a fan shape can direct the canes. Or, erect a trellis or lattice frame and anchor the canes with horticultural tape ties. If designed with hinges, it can be removed for house painting and regular maintenance. Consider using either 'New Dawn' or double-pink 'Zephirine Drouhin'.

PILLARS AND STANDARDS

A number of varieties perform wonderfully if trained to wrap around a pillar or post. This allows you the freedom to create columns of

color arising from mixed beds and borders. Do not use true climbers for this purpose, as they are often too large and vigorous. Try the pillar-type varieties such as red 'Don Juan', yellow 'Golden Showers', or multi-colored 'Joseph's Coat'. Alternatively, use a standard tree version of your favorite hybrid tea, floribunda, or miniature to create a vertical effect within a bed of perennials.

ARBORS AND PERGOLAS

What more perfect way to use roses in a garden setting than with a rose-laden archway as an entrance. Plant two or more bushes of the same variety on either side of an arbor or archway and train their canes to go over the top and down the other side. This marriage of canes from both sides of the archway produces a magnificent display of roses all the way around the arbor. This concept can be expanded using a pergola- or gazebo-type structure. A length of pathway can be lined and covered with a series of arbors that creates a virtual tunnel of roses in the garden. Imagine a walk down a rose-draped pathway, rich with the fragrance of 'Zephirine Drouhin', with sunlight streaming through the skylight of soft pink roses.

SHOUT IT FROM THE ROOFTOPS

Some unique varieties of roses love to ramble on their own up into trees— even over the rooftops of houses. These so-called ramblers usually need very little maintenance (or spent-blossom removal in order to promote additional flowering cycles). If you have adequate space, consider trying one of these varieties for best effect—the pink climbing polyantha 'Mlle Cecile Brunner', or the soft pink 'Paul's Himalayan Musk'.

A perfect backdrop for deep-pink 'Parade' is the climbing polyantha 'China Doll', (above), which has been grown on 6-foot stock to create the effect of a pink-blooming weeping willow.

Allowing a rambler like 'Wedding Day' to pervade and use a tree for support (below) is another great idea for creating vertical color in the garden.

TOP CLIMBERS

'Altissimo': red, single-petaled
'America': orange and pink, double
'Autumn Sunset': apricot, double
'Berries 'n' Cream': deep pink
    striped, double
'Dublin Bay': medium red, double
'Fourth of July': red striped
'Mlle Cecile Brunner': light pink, pompon
'Joseph's Coat': red blend, double
'New Dawn': light pink, double
'Sombreuil': white flat, very double
'Zephirine Drouhin': medium pink, double

The romance of roses in containers: A simple hanging basket of 'Woman's Day' (left) adds charm and color to a bare wall; 'Pretty Polly' provides a moveable visual feast in an elegant container on a patio (center); and the disease-resistant floribunda 'Flower Carpet' (right) produces a profusion of pink blossoms along a pathway.

Create an inviting destination for quiet contemplation by surrounding a simple stone bench with containers of miniatures, floribundas, and hybrid tea roses (below). Growing roses in containers on a terrace or patio is a welcome addition to the plants in the beds and borders of the garden, but for balconies and some city gardens, this may be the only way to grow roses successfully.

Consider Small Spaces

There are a number of simple and effective ways to introduce roses to small spaces. Try a rose bush beside your mailbox. The clean white floribunda, 'Iceberg', is an attractive choice. On the entry steps to the house, place a few roses in containers to make a bold statement and to make the front entry more inviting to visitors. On the patio, pots of roses lend color and scent, plus they beautify the setting.

For a small space, miniature roses are ideal. Grown in containers or planted as borders around the garden or patio, they bring a range of color (and growing habits) to a small space. Plant the miniature 'Sweet Chariot' in a hanging basket, for instance, and it will fill the patio with perfume as well as its deep-mauve color. Use miniature tree roses in containers to amplify height and bring diversity. Miniature roses can be planted in just about any type of container—given a south- or west-facing exposure on a deck, patio, or balcony—adding a distinctly personal touch to your outdoor living space.

Create a garden on the patio by grouping pots and containers in clusters. Experiment with containers in different arrangements to achieve the best complementary color display.

Rearranging roses in containers—much like rearranging your living room furniture—is an added bonus that rose growers wish they could bring to the garden. With the range and diversity of roses, you can try out the most ambitious color schemes and change them all the very next day if you wish!

PLANTS FOR SMALL SPACES

FLORIBUNDAS
'Amber Queen': apricot blend, double
'Blueberry Hill': mauve, double
'Iceberg': white, double
'Purple Tiger': mauve, double
'Sunsprite': deep yellow, double

MINIATURES
'Gourmet Popcorn': white
'Child's Play': white blend, double
'Jean Kenneally': apricot blend, double
'Party Girl': yellow blend, double
'Why Not': red with yellow eye

The double, cupped, coppery-pink blossoms of the rambler 'Albertine' start out with salmon-red buds (left). Excellent for a fence or pergola, this rose may be allowed to form a broad, sprawling shrub. Here, its arching, blossom-laden stems have been trained to trail across a rooftop balcony, beckoning visitors below with its rich, sweet fragrance.

'The Fairy', here in an oak barrel (above left), is unsurpassed for its abundance of small pink double flowers and its stamina. Make the most of the miniature 'Rainbow's End' by planting with silver-leaved perennials like snow-in-summer (left). Combine pots of roses with attractive annuals (above) on decks and patios.

Companion Plants for Roses

*I*t used to be that roses were relegated to their own corner of the garden. This Victorian attitude left nothing to show in the rose garden but canes and barren earth for most of the year. Thankfully, roses are now integrated with the rest of the garden, sharing space with garden plants of every size, shape, and texture. With their arching growth pattern, roses welcome companion plants growing through and around them. Roses, in fact, can grow and mix well nearly anywhere in the landscape.

In your overall garden plan, any plant—whether it's an annual, bulb, perennial, shrub, herb, grass, vine, or small tree—can be combined with roses to dynamic effect. When selecting companion plants, consider color, shape, texture, size, and how these elements will enhance or detract from your strategy. Companion plants can fill the ground spaces in and around roses while providing a continuous harmony of color throughout the year. They insert color between rose bloom cycles and provide structure to the landscape. For example, annuals are available in a multitude of colors to contrast with or complement your choice of roses. Perennials and vines extend the season of bloom and

A gallery of unusual combination plantings for roses in the landscape (clockwise from top left): climber 'Aloha' underplanted with silver-leaved artemisias; the pale violet blossoms of milky bellflower create a lovely foil for red and white roses in the mixed border; creamy-white boxleaf honeysuckle, purple catmint, and blue salvia square off with 'Festival'; chartreuse lady's mantle and hardy geranium make a striking underplanting for the climber 'Danse de Feu'; the scarlet-crimson blossoms of 'Festival' combine wonderfully with golden hops, rose campion, and stalks of yellow mullein.

COMPANION PLANTS

WITH WHITE ROSES:
Boxwood
  (Buxus)
Garden pinks
  (Dianthus plumarius)
Stonecrop
  (Sedum spurium)
Lady's mantle
  (Alchemilla vulgaris)
Milky bellflower
  (Campanula lactiflora)
Snow-in-summer
  (Cerastium tomentosum)
Wormwood
  (Artemisia)
Lavender cotton
  (Santolina chamaecyparissus)
Baby's breath
  (Gypsophila paniculata)
Lamb's ear
  (Stachys lanata)

WITH RED ROSES:
Stonecrop
  (Sedum album)
Dalmatian bellflower
  (Campanula portenschlagiana)
Catmint
  (Nepeta)
Lavender
  (Lavandula)
Larkspur
  (Consolida ajacis)

often provide an architectural element, as do ornamental grasses. Contrasting foliage plants and herbs can create a pleasing textural counterpoint in the rose garden.

The possibilities are endless and completely up to the individual. Find out what works for you and your garden. Work with familiar plants from a local nursery or garden center. In cooler areas, consider spring-flowering bulbs that are winter hardy. Of course, the most popular combination plant with roses is clematis, which twines and climbs throughout the rose's foliage, filling holes with bright, starry blossoms of color. Contrasting foliage textures and colors work especially well. And don't forget annuals such as pansies, petunias, and marigolds, the old standbys that fill in blank spaces throughout the summer months.

Remember, creating complementary color combinations is a matter of personal taste. There are no hard and fast rules. If, after a while, you decide something doesn't work as expected, you can always move the offending plant and try it somewhere else. Rules, after all, are made to be broken. But if you need a place to start in order to successfully mix combination plants with roses, consult the lists of suggestions on these pages. With a little bit of luck and imagination, you'll create lovely mixes of texture and color.

COMPANION PLANTS

WITH YELLOW ROSES:
Catmint
  (*Nepeta*)
Lavender
  (*Lavandula*)
Licorice plant
  (*Helichrysum petiolare*)
Creeping thyme
  (*Thymus serpyllum*)
Lamb's ear
  (*Stachys lanata*)

WITH PINK ROSES:
Stonecrop
  (*Sedum album*)
Lady's mantle
  (*Alchemilla vulgaris*)
Bellflowers
  (*Campanula*)
Diascia
  (*Diascia rigescens*)
Hardy geranium
  (*Geranium sanguineum*)
Wooly thyme
  (*Thymus pseudolanuginosus*)
Lamb's ear
  (*Stachys lanata*)
Catmint
  (*Nepeta*)
Plumbago
  (*Ceratostigma*)
Lavender
  (*Lavandula*)

Compact floribunda hedge 'Simplicity' and Peruvian lily.

Climbing 'Maigold' mingles with Clematis montana.

Pink 'Rita' with blue salvia and wallflower.

'Old Blush' China rose with Geranium 'Johnson's Blue'.

Old garden rose 'Mme Isaac Pereire' and Clematis 'Henryi'.

Rose 'Graham Thomas' and Clematis 'Ville de Lyon'.

Perfect pair: Rose 'Amber Queen' matches lily 'Luxor'.

Echo effect: Striped roses interplanted with spirea.

Soft rose-pink 'Bonica' and diascia.

Rose Gardens

Planning the Smaller Rose Garden

A small rose garden planted and tended by a novice rosarian can provide maximum impact and pleasure. Site location is vital. Select an area that gets at least six hours of sunshine a day. This can be an open area that will become an island of flowers, or an area along a wall, fence, or pathway. Plan your colors, then select varieties from our list of sturdy, disease-resistant, easy-to-grow roses for beginners.

HOW TO DESIGN AN ISLAND

An island bed can be a circular, rectangular, or free-form design that follows contours in the landscape. It is typically surrounded by lawn. The center of the bed should be the tallest focal point. Standard tree roses, which are about 6 feet tall, command attention. Floribunda standards tend to make more massive displays of flowers in limited space than the one-bloom-per-stem hybrid tea. However, if a hybrid tea standard is the centerpiece, place a surrounding row of hybrid tea bushes about two to three feet apart. Finish off the design with a perimeter of floribundas. If the central standard tree is a floribunda, continue with a surrounding circle

TOP VARIETIES FOR BEGINNERS

HYBRID TEAS
'Kardinal'
'St. Patrick'
'Brigadoon'
'Signature'
'Valencia'

FLORIBUNDAS
'Amber Queen'
'Iceberg'
'Showbiz'
'Sheila's Perfume'
'Sexy Rexy'

MINIATURES
'Behold'
'Gourmet Popcorn'
'Luis Desamero'
'Minnie Pearl'
'Old Glory'

OLD GARDEN ROSES
'Baronne Prevost'
'Irene Watts'
'La Belle Sultane'
'Paul Neyron'
'Sombreuil'

SHRUBS/ENGLISH ROSES
'Carefree Delight'
'Hansa'
'Golden Celebration'
'Perdita'
'Tamora'

CLIMBERS
'Altissimo'
'Berries 'n' Cream'
'New Dawn'

The simplest rose garden designs involve a circular bed planted with hybrid teas in the center, surrounded by floribundas (below left). Another approach is to use rectangular beds, like this raised terrace bed (below), filled with just one or two varieties of roses.

For a small formal garden, combine roses, annuals, and perennials in a mixed bed, anchor it with boxwood, and use a classic stone urn as its centerpiece (above). Irregular curves (right) create depth and added interest.

of floribundas, followed by a row of miniatures. Fill in with your favorite companion plants and you have created a breathtaking masterpiece.

CREATE DRAMA AT THE FOUNDATION

Roses are ideal shrubs for foundation planting. Selection should be determined in large part by the depth of the bed. For instance, if the depth of the bed is 4 feet or less, a single row of floribundas all of the same variety will provide a massive display of flowers. If the bed is 5 feet or more deep, consider using climbers against the wall that will intertwine their canes on a trellis. Use a row of modern shrub roses in front of the climbers, and finish off the entire design with some choice medium-size floribundas in the front.

Color makes the overall design succeed. Contrasting colors such as red, yellow, and white make dramatic displays. Delicate pinks and whites create a softer look. Consider well the color of the wall behind when choosing rose varieties. Cerise and magenta, for example, tend to clash with the warm tones of brick; a better choice might be orange or salmon. Mix colors for a more relaxed, informal effect. Or use a monochromatic scheme for greater formality.

Perhaps the most common use of roses is to plant them along the foundation of a house (left), where they soften the landscape, such as hybrid musk 'Prosperity' (below left). Floribundas embrace a garden gate (below) to welcome visitors.

The Larger Rose Garden

Once you have enjoyed a small rose garden, you may be ready to move on to a larger one. The large rose garden is loaded with creative possibilities. With adequate space available, the full diversity of classes, shapes, sizes, color, and forms of roses take center stage. Access for maintenance will be necessary, so keep that in mind. Large gardens often use mass plantings of one or two varieties to create a colorful, dramatic display (a welcome sight along walkways leading to the front door). Simple designs are often the most successful. Contour the shape of the rose beds to suit your house and its surroundings. Your choice may be square, rectangular, circular, curved, long, or short—there are no limits. Unreel your garden hose and experiment with various shapes and curves until you find one that is pleasing. If you have a large tree in the garden, consider planting 'Mlle Cecile Brunner' so it can scramble up its trunk.

can be covered with climbers, ramblers, and some large shrubs. If the bed is adjacent to a wall, take a step back to gain a larger perspective. Achieve a terraced effect with miniatures occupying the front of the border areas. Planting different varieties at various heights creates interest. Remember that standard 3-foot tree roses can be used quite effectively, but in cold climates where roses need winter protection, standards require some protection before freezing temperatures set in. The recent availability of weeping tree roses (grafted onto either 48- or 60-inch-tall stock) also allows you to create impressive displays within beds using varieties known to spread out and bloom in large clusters. Adventuresome gardeners should try 'Carefree Delight' (winner of the All America Rose Selection), as well as the pink polyantha, 'The Fairy', or the award-winning white miniature, 'Gourmet Popcorn', all available as 48-inch weeping standard tree roses.

Clipped boxwood hedges frame floribunda 'Iceberg' in a large formal garden (below); densely planted hybrid teas and grandifloras provide summer-long color that is unsurpassed (below center); bourbon roses, such as 'Louise Odier' (below right) bloom intermittently throughout the season, as in this irregularly shaped border.

HOW TO USE SIZE AND SHAPE

Decide which types of roses are best suited to your plans based on the locations of the beds and their proximity to structures. For instance, walls, fences, trellises, and arbors

HOW TO USE COLOR AND FORM

Color sets the mood of the rose garden. Bright, vibrant colors create excitement; pastels create a sense of peace. Contrasting colors are stimulating; complementary colors

have a calming effect. Decide which color effect you want to achieve. Where white is the predominant color in a rose bed, you may want to include mauve, light pink, yellow, or orange. For a dominantly red rose bed, consider light pink, deep pink, coral pink, or white. For a tranquil setting using mostly medium pink roses, complement the monochromatic color scheme with light pink, deep pink, and light mauve.

A large garden is the perfect opportunity to display a wide variety of flower forms. The free-blooming, cluster-flowered floribundas offer massive displays of blooms. Modern shrub roses are available in so many shapes and sizes that they mix beautifully with suitable companion plants to create the look of an English cottage garden. Whatever you decide, take advantage of underused outdoor spaces and fill them with roses!

Stair-step a rose garden in front of a wall by planting a pink climber against it with two red standard tree roses and two red hybrid teas in front (right). Complete the design with a white floribunda in the center and a row of pink miniature roses. Boxwood hedges define both intimate paths and garden space in a rear yard given over wholly to roses (below left). Expanses of lawn between several island beds (below right) create a generous, even luxurious mood.

Large Formal Rose Gardens

While designing large formal rose gardens, several considerations come into play. Traditionally, roses are the only plants used in the overall design. Clipped boxwood hedges are often used to frame the beds. Fountains and sculptures can add yet another dimension to the landscape. But above all, the main design of the garden typically has a geometric symmetry with more than one focal point. Planning for this type of garden takes a great deal of organization. While few gardeners embark on such ambitious projects, these same design elements may be successfully translated into more reasonably scaled gardens.

GEOMETRY AND SYMMETRY

Well-planned and executed, a formal rose garden can bring a surprising organization to the home landscape, as well as a stunning framework for roses of all types and colors. Laid out with an eye to symmetry and order, it can reflect and amplify the perfect form and symmetry of the rose blossom itself. Clearly defined borders increase the garden's sense of geometry. And because the formal rose garden is balanced from all angles, it can provide both rest and drama for the eye.

HOW TO USE FOCAL POINTS

A garden's focal point is its visual center of attention. It is easy to create focal points with a sculpture, waterfall, or even a small fountain. Such features are welcome additions that provide visual interest within the rose-filled landscape, especially when plant heights are similar. Incorporate a garden ornament in your landscape and see how pleasing its effect can be. Water features—such as a fountain, running stream, or pond—add charm and a soul-soothing effect to any garden.

The many faces of formal: Climbing rose 'New Dawn' forms a canopy over a red-brick walkway between boxwood parterres (top left), creating a refuge from the sun. A massive display of roses designed in radiating ripples of color (center left) continues the circular form of a central water feature. A series of carefully laid out beds, edged with clipped boxwood and surrounded by gravel paths (below left), allows visitors to this formal garden a chance to view examples of bush, standard, and climbing roses in all styles and varieties. The pink rose in the foreground is 'Century Two'.

A brilliant blaze of 'Sun Flare' brightens up this formal rose garden at Huntington Gardens in San Marino, California. It is backed by a pergola covered with a breathtaking variety of climbers and ramblers in every color imaginable. Most of the old wood on the roses growing on the pergola is removed after the once-yearly flowering, and the new wood trained in its place. This keeps the walkways tidy so that visitors can walk through without becoming caught on wayward shoots.

Ready, Set, Grow

Buying Roses

By the time you've selected a rose plant for your garden, it already has an extensive history. It begins in a nursery field, which is planted with a cutting of a rootstock or understock—the base of the plant—and tended for one year. Common varieties used as rootstocks are 'Dr. Huey', 'Manetti', 'Odorata', 'Multiflora', and 'Fortuniana'. (Make a note: Rootstock names may help later when choosing a rose that will survive your winter climate.) Next, the chosen variety is budded onto the shank of the rootstock. After one year, the growth above the bud is removed and the variety develops for another year. Finally, the roses are harvested, graded, refrigerated, and shipped to nurseries and garden centers.

You can purchase roses locally, through mail-order sources—even at discount stores and groceries. It's best, of course, to buy your plants only from a supplier who guarantees their quality, not from a store where roses are an afterthought. Pre-packaged, bare-root plants have a tendency to dry out, and the retail atmosphere may cause early growth.

Roses are graded according to a uniform standard. A top grade No. 1 hybrid tea, grandiflora, or climber must have at least three strong canes $5/16$ inch in diameter, which branch no higher than 3 inches above the bud union. Grade No. 1 polyanthas must have four canes of that diameter. Cane lengths vary for each type: 15 inches for floribundas, 18 inches for hybrid teas, and 24 inches for climbers. A rose graded No. $1\frac{1}{2}$ must have 2 stems $5/16$-inch in diameter. Cane lengths for No. $1\frac{1}{2}$ grade roses are shorter.

Try to buy only grade No. 1 roses. The time and effort required for a lower grade rose—and your potential disappointment in its performance—far outweighs any savings.

How to Grade Bare-Root Roses: *Of the three bare-root roses pictured above, the top two are given a grade of No. 1 because they have 3 or more canes measuring at least $5/16$-inch in diameter. The lowest bare-root rose is given a grade of No. $1\frac{1}{2}$ because it has only two canes of the minimum diameter. Note the range in No. 1-graded bare-root roses. The rose at the top is superior, it has a good network of fibrous roots and a strong union where the top growth joins the rootstock.*

Fields of Roses: *Each year, more than 25 million rose plants are grown in the fields of Wasco, California, just north of Bakersfield. After harvesting they will be sold as bare-root plants. The region's sandy loam and mild climate is ideal for propagating roses.*

HOW TO CHOOSE ROSES IN A TUBE

Roses sold in tubes usually have their roots and canes trimmed to fit—both for convenience and for easy transportation. The number, diameter, condition, and height of the canes are visible, but the root system (usually packed in wood shavings) is not. Inspect the canes as you would a bare-root plant, checking for health, vigor, and form. Because the plastic case is like a small hothouse, it can encourage premature growth. Look for wrinkled skin—a sure sign of dehydration. Once you get a packaged bare-root rose home, remove the plastic and store it in a cool, moist medium.

Suppliers sell roses as bare-root, packaged bare-root (sometimes called a "tube"), or container-grown. Bare-root roses are usually less expensive than those in containers, and since nurseries normally stock them in moist sawdust, you can inspect their roots and canes.

Look carefully before you buy. Inspect plants for sturdy, fibrous, well-branched roots and firm, green canes. Avoid plants that look dry or shriveled, are not well shaped, or show signs of disease (swelling, deformities, and discolorations). And steer clear of plants with premature growth. These have begun to pull out of dormancy and are using up the nutrients they'll need to get started in your garden. Plant your newly purchased bare-root roses as soon as possible. If you do have to store them, keep them cool and moist, in sawdust or peat moss.

Container-grown roses can remain in their containers until it's time to plant. When you plant depends on both the type of rose purchased and on where you live. Bare-root roses will be available when they're dormant and you can plant them when the ground is not frozen. In the South, where winter temperatures stay above 10° F, plant your bare-root roses in the first months of the year. Where winters get cold, wait until after all danger of frost has passed. Although planting season for container-grown roses can be as late as summer, it's best to start them in the spring, so their roots have a chance to get established before summer heat sets in.

CHOOSING CONTAINER-GROWN ROSES

Though you may find fewer varieties and pay more for container-grown roses (primarily because of their heavier weight and increased shipping costs), they offer certain advantages. Because they are in active growth, and often in bloom, you can readily verify their vigor, color, bloom size, and fragrance. They're also relatively easy to plant. Some nurseries will plant their unsold spring stock and some will stock container-grown plants throughout the year. After midsummer, they're more likely to have become root-bound, and thus more difficult to establish in the garden. Examine the plant carefully. The same grading standards and signs of health apply, and there should be no die-back or twiggy growth, a sign it has been in the container for too long. Avoid root-bound plants (ask the nursery staff to remove the pot for you) and roses planted in less than 5-gallon pots—their roots may have been pruned severely to fit their containers.

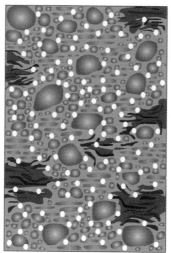

In the left diagram, water (shaded blue) travels slowly through dense clay, creating an environment too low in oxygen for rose roots. At far right, porous sand allows water to pass through quickly, leaving the soil too dry. In the center, the correct proportion of sand, organic matter, and clay provides both oxygen and water for healthy roots.

Soil and Site

Roses that grow well—with a minimum of care and maintenance—are those that have been carefully chosen to match their site. Climate is the first consideration. Before you make your final selections, find out your hardiness zone. It is a measure of how cold winters can be in your particular region of the country. Roses are labeled with the zones in which they'll most likely survive the winter cold (see pages 52 and 53 for information on hardiness zones).

Before you plant your roses, carefully consider the proposed site. Look at your potential garden spots with an eye toward the ideal location, but don't panic if you can't find it. Roses are more adaptable than they've been given credit for.

Roses like sunlight—at least six hours of it each day, so select a location that won't fall into the shade of overhanging trees or buildings. (No rose likes shade, but a few will tolerate it better than most. See "Roses More Tolerant of Shade," page 43.) Roses also need good air circulation (but not wind) in order to keep their foliage dry and to resist disease. Roses do not take well to competition for water and nutrients, so be sure to plant them well away from greedy tree roots and shrubs.

SOIL TEXTURE AND STRUCTURE

Get to know your soil. Grab a handful (moist material works best), and squeeze it into a ball. Release it: Clay soil will stick together, sandy soil will fall apart, and silty soil will feel greasy. If the ball holds its shape, but crumbles under a little finger-poking, you have sandy loam—the very best soil for growing roses.

The texture is important because it affects how easily the roots can absorb water and oxygen. Clay soils won't take in water well, and when they are saturated, they won't release it. This keeps the roots from obtaining oxygen. Sandy soils drain too quickly, robbing the roots of moisture and nutrients. The proper texture for roses is a mix of the three main soil ingredients (sand, clay, and humus,

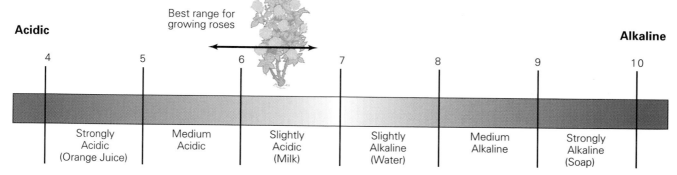

Best range for growing roses

Acidic   **Alkaline**

| 4 | 5 | 6 | 7 | 8 | 9 | 10 |

Strongly Acidic (Orange Juice)   Medium Acidic   Slightly Acidic (Milk)   Slightly Alkaline (Water)   Medium Alkaline   Strongly Alkaline (Soap)

Soil pH: *Roses grow best in soils with a pH range of 5.8 to 6.8 (slightly acidic) because they can absorb nutrients efficiently. At extreme pH values, plants suffer from improper nutrition and will be stunted. High acidity levels (below pH 5.8) will produce yellow foliage on the entire plant. High alkalinity (above 6.8) produces yellow leaves at the top of plants.*

in proportions of roughly one-third each), which strikes just the right balance between adequate drainage and nutrient and water retention. And although it may not seem easy, you can make soil with the right texture if yours is not ideal. A mix of equal parts of your native soil (for clay and a little sand), peat moss (a great humus source), and potting soil (for supplemental sand and humus) will closely approximate sandy loam.

ACIDITY AND ALKALINITY

While soil texture can have a profound influence on the vigor and productivity of a rose, so also can its pH—a measure of its acidity and alkalinity. Soil pH is measured in a scale running from 0 to 14, with a value of 7 considered neutral. Anything below pH 7 is acidic and above pH 7 is alkaline. The acidity or alkalinity of the soil is important because it affects the rate at which plants absorb nutrients. If the soil is too acid or too alkaline, nutrient intake is reduced and the rose will not thrive. Roses do well in soils that are within a pH range of 5.8 to 6.8 You can't measure your soil by grabbing a handful, but you can test it yourself (with a monitor available at your garden center) or have it tested by your county extension service.

If the soil is too acidic (less than pH 5.8), add lime (½ cup per 9 cubic feet, which is about the space of one hybrid tea rose); if the soil is too alkaline, add 1 teaspoon of sulfur per 9 cubic feet. (Check with your local extension agent or garden center to find the best sources of each for your region.) Floribundas need less (¼ cup lime, ½ teaspoon sulfur), and miniatures still less (⅛ cup lime and ¼ cup sulfur). Add pH amendments when making your rose bed, or immediately before planting single roses according to our instructions.

ALLOW ROOM TO GROW

And finally, remember this: Have some sort of plan before you plant. You'll need to fertilize these roses and prune them when they're fully grown, and you can't do this properly if they're spaced too close together. Allow enough room so that you can access the center of the planting from at least one side. Consider the ultimate size of the plant. Hybrid teas and grandifloras should be planted 2 to 2½ feet apart (3 to 4 feet in mild climates). Floribundas need less room, 1½ to 2 feet (2 to 3 feet in mild climates). Plant miniatures 1 to 3 feet apart, depending on the variety and climate. And plant species, shrubs and old garden roses 5 to 6 feet apart (up to twice that distance in mild climates).

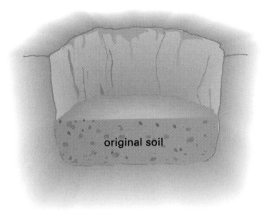

Dig the Hole:
Dig a hole 2 feet wide and 2 feet deep. Test its drainage by filling it up with water. Water should disappear within several hours (if not, the soil may be high in clay). Replace one-third of the original soil back into the hole.

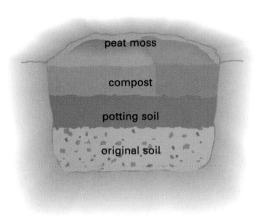

Add the Amendments:
Next, fill the hole by another third with a good commercial potting soil. Finally, fill the remainder of the hole with a mixture of two parts organic compost and one part peat moss.

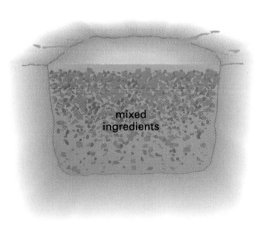

Prepare the Soil:
Thoroughly mix all ingredients and water well. Let the hole stand for about seven days, watering every two days. This waiting period allows the bacteria that fix nitrogen to build up again.

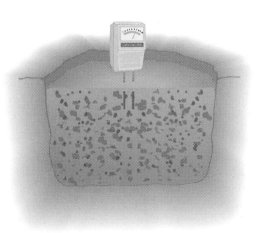

Test the Mixture:
The soil level in the hole will settle an inch or two. Before planting, test the soil with a pH meter. It should measure 5.8 to 6.8. If necessary, add lime to raise pH or sulfur to lower pH and bring it into the proper range.

Plant the Rose:
Set aside most of the soil. Form a cone in the bottom of the hole with the remaining soil. Use a broom handle to make sure that the bud union is at the correct level. Carefully fan out the roots over the cone of soil.

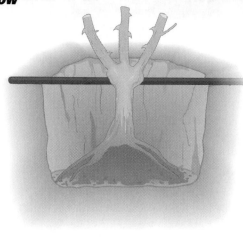

Add the Soil Mixture:
Slowly add the reserved soil to cover the roots. Do not compress the soil on top of the roots. Leave about 4 inches from the top of the hole still to be filled in.

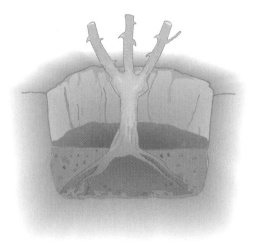

Natural Soil Settling:
Add water to allow a slow and gentle settling of the soil. Water several times to let the soil fill in completely. Add the remaining soil and water once more.

The Final Touch:
Mound the exposed bud union with mulch to prevent moisture loss. Create a dam of soil around the plant to collect water. Roots will be established in a few weeks and the mound can be removed.

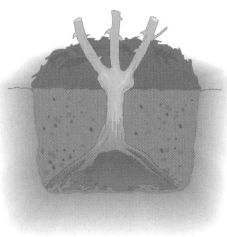

Planting Bare Roots

Most often, roses, whether old or modern, arrive in your garden as dormant, bare-root plants, but they can also be purchased as potted, container-grown specimens. You can purchase bare-root roses at a local nursery or order them by mail. A bare-root rose looks stark, with stubby, thorny stems and stiff roots growing in the opposite direction from a rough knob. The knob is the graft union, where the roots and main stem were grafted together. (Many old garden roses are grown on their own roots and do not have a graft union.)

These bare roots need a good soaking in water before you stick them in the ground—they need to store up moisture that can be lost during the planting process. So soak them for two to three hours in a vitamin B-1 solution ($\frac{1}{2}$ ounce to a gallon; available at your local garden center). Next, trim off any broken roots, but avoid trimming the canes unless they are damaged. Fresh cuts allow moisture to escape. If any canes are damaged, however, cut them and seal them with a dab of white glue.

HOW TO PREPARE THE HOLE

With the advance work done—including the soil preparation steps on the previous page—you're ready to plant your roses. First, remove most of the soil from the prepared planting hole. Make a cone of soil in the center to accommodate the roots and spread them out evenly over the cone (if one or two roots are too long, trim them to fit the hole.) Check the height of the bud union with a broomstick laid across the hole and adjust the cone of soil to keep the bud union at the correct level for your climate. As a rule of thumb, plant the bud union 2 to 3 inches below ground in cold winter climates (winter lows below −10° F), and at ground level or slightly above where winter lows are between −10° and +10° F and warmer.

Add the remaining soil, firming it as you go, and water it with the vitamin B-1 solution to help it settle in. Mound the plant with 8 to 12 inches of mulch, and encircle it with a dam of soil to help collect water. Water it well every three to four days to get the roots off to a healthy start. When the root structure is established (in about three weeks), remove the mound a little at a time. In four to five weeks the bud eyes should be swollen and about to burst. Watch for wrinkling on the canes—the first sign of dehydration. If this occurs, recut the canes below the wrinkling, remound the plant, and water well.

Planting Container-Grown Roses

Planting container-grown roses has become increasingly popular; they can be planted not only during bare-root season, but also later on in the season. Container-grown roses are also somewhat easier to plant—you don't need to make the cone of soil for the roots, for example.

Before you plant a container-grown rose, gradually reduce its water (a process called hardening off) for a week. But on the day you plant, make sure the container soil (and the soil in the planting hole) is moist. Reducing its water beforehand will help prepare the rose for the transplant, and watering at planting time will help keep the root ball together and reduce stress caused by the surrounding dry ground soil absorbing moisture away from the roots.

Follow the simple steps below for removing the container and planting the rose bush. Remember to keep the bud union at the height it would be if it were a bare-root plant. Refill the planting hole with soil dug from it. Press the soil gently around the root ball, but do not stamp it with your feet. Be sure to water well until the roots are well established.

Remove the Bottom:
Lay the container on its side. Cut off the base of the compressed fiber pot with a small saw. Try not to damage any of the roots.

Place in Hole:
Place the root ball in the hole that has been dug out to about 2 feet wide and 2 feet deep. Make sure the bud union is at the proper level.

Remove the Container:
Remove the rest of the compressed fiber pot as if you were peeling an orange. Don't worry if some roots show on the surface of the root ball.

Fill in with Soil:
Fill the remaining space with a good quality potting soil or amended soil. Water, allow to settle, and finish off with more potting soil.

Planting in Containers

SUGGESTED VARIETIES FOR CONTAINER-GROWN ROSES

HYBRID TEAS
'First Prize'
'Ingrid Bergman'
'Olympiad'

FLORIBUNDAS
'French Lace'
'Iceberg'
'Purple Tiger'

MINIATURES
'Gourmet Popcorn'
'Glowing Amber'
'Hot Tamale'
'Party Girl'

OLD GARDEN ROSES
'Baronne Prevost'
'Paul Neyron'
'Reine Victoria'

A water ring is a convenient way to provide roses in containers with a slow, steady supply of water. The soil is completely soaked in only five minutes.

I f you're short on outdoor garden space or simply want to decorate a patio, deck, or terrace, grow roses in containers. The wide variety of color, shape, blossom, and portability of roses provides endless solutions to small-space garden problems.

Start by choosing the proper container—not only for its looks, but for its size and composition, as well. The right size matters—the container will be home to the rose for many years to come. No matter what kind of container you choose, make sure it has adequate drainage. Drill holes if it doesn't. Rose roots rot if they stand in water. You can grow bare-root roses in containers, but roses purchased as container-grown plants seem to adapt better—perhaps because they're already used to this environment.

Roses grown in containers, like those that are garden grown, need soil that is well drained and nutrient retentive. You can make your own from three parts loam and one part organic matter. Ready-mixed synthetic soils work well also. Add the soil mix to the container, and whether the rose is bare root or container grown, adjust the soil depth so that the top of the plant is 1½ to 2 inches below the top of the container (you'll need the extra space to keep water from overflowing). Add the remaining soil to this depth, pack it tightly to eliminate air pockets, then soak it thoroughly. You can mulch your container or plant it with a shallow-rooted ground cover or seedling annuals.

Place the container in a location where it will get six hours of daily sun, and turn it now and then if it starts tilting to the light.

Because containers have less soil than gardens (and therefore a smaller nutrient and moisture base), roses grown in them will need more frequent fertilizing and watering.

Every three years or so, the container soil will become worn out—nutrient depleted. That's when it's time to replant—at the same time you would prune it (see "Pruning," page 44). Remove the root ball from the pot and trim off 2 to 3 inches from its sides and bottom. Replant in the same container, using fresh soil mix.

Original root ball

Main root system

Fine feeder roots

Amended soil

Soil polymer

Drainage hole

Saucer

TIPS FOR CONTAINER GARDENING

Make sure containers have holes for proper drainage. Four holes of about ¼ inch diameter should be sufficient for a 1-gallon container. For larger containers, holes may be larger.

A tip to reduce watering containers: Expand a level tablespoon of soil polymer in a glass of water for 20 minutes. Incorporate it into the soil for a 5-gallon pot before planting.

Consider planting roses in containers that feature a built-in reservoir at the bottom that holds water without soaking the roots. Shown here is the miniature rose, 'Behold'.

SELECTING A CONTAINER

Plastic pots are light and inexpensive (don't buy black, which in warm climates can soak up heat and burn roots). Porous terra-cotta lets moisture travel through its walls, as does wood. The evaporation keeps roots cool, but plants may need more frequent watering. There are terra-cotta glazed containers, terra-cotta look-alikes (made of vinyl), and decorative ceramic pots. Keep in mind that ceramic and terra-cotta will crack if left outside in cold-winter areas. Large whisky barrels make excellent containers, as long as they have adequate drainage holes. All pots may become heavy when planted with roses, so equip them with casters if you can.

Miniature roses are best in containers in the 5- to 7-gallon range, wider than they are tall (their roots tend to grow out, not down). Larger roses need more room (15 to 20 gallons) to keep from becoming root bound.

Simple Steps to *Healthy Roses*

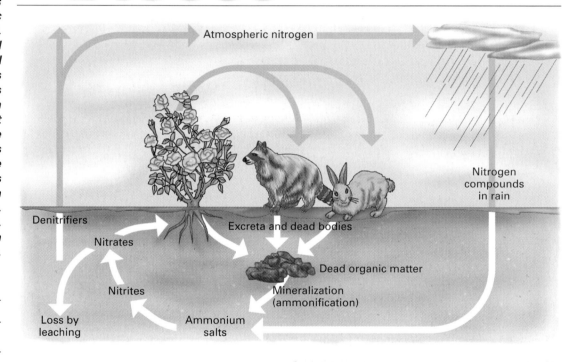

Feeding Roses

Well-fed roses not only reach their full size and produce abundant flowers, they also stay healthy and resist attack from insects and diseases. What you feed your roses, and how often, will depend to some extent on your soil. Roses grown in sandy soil may need more frequent feeding than those grown in loam or heavier soil.

Roses need three primary nutrients—nitrogen (the "N" on a fertilizer label), phosphorous (P) and potassium (K)—as well as a number of secondary and trace elements in order to thrive. Nitrogen promotes foliage growth; phosphorous, healthy root and flower development; and potassium maintains vigor. Calcium, magnesium, and sulphur (secondary elements) and trace elements (boron, chlorine, copper, and iron) also promote plant-cell and root growth.

Primary nutrients are available from both organic (derived from plant or animal life)

ORGANIC VS. INORGANIC

Organic sources (composts, manures, and cotton-seed meal) take 4 to 10 weeks or longer before they are sufficiently decomposed by soil bacteria to make their nutrients available to the plant. On the other hand, synthetic or inorganic fertilizers make their nutrients immediately available to the root system. Synthetic nutrients are depleted more rapidly and may require more frequent applications. Time-release synthetics are specially formulated to deliver nutrients at a slow, steady rate.

and synthetic or inorganic materials. Synthetic fertilizers come in dry, liquid, or foliar liquid form. Work dry fertilizers into the soil (moisten the soil first) and water it after application to carry the nutrients to the roots. Liquid fertilizers are added to water with an in-hose applicator,

HOW TO READ A LABEL

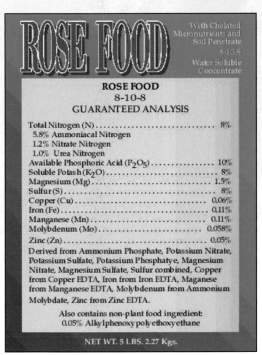

ROSE FOOD
8-10-8
GUARANTEED ANALYSIS

Total Nitrogen (N)	8%
5.8% Ammoniacal Nitrogen	
1.2% Nitrate Nitrogen	
1.0% Urea Nitrogen	
Available Phosphoric Acid (P_2O_5)	10%
Soluble Potash (K_2O)	8%
Magnesium (Mg)	1.5%
Sulfur (S)	8%
Copper (Cu)	0.06%
Iron (Fe)	0.11%
Manganese (Mn)	0.11%
Molybdenum (Mo)	0.058%
Zinc (Zn)	0.05%

Derived from Ammonium Phosphate, Potassium Nitrate, Potassium Sulfate, Potassium Phosphatye, Magnesium Nitrate, Magnesium Sulfate, Sulfur combined, Copper from Copper EDTA, Iron from Iron EDTA, Maganese from Manganese EDTA, Molybdenum from Ammonium Molybdate, Zinc from Zinc EDTA.

Also contains non-plant food ingredient: 0.05% Alkylphenoxypolyethoxyethane

NET WT. 5 LBS. 2.27 Kgs.

A Guaranteed Analysis statement must appear on all mixed fertilizer labels. The label must indicate the proportion of each element present, as well as its sources (in this example, ammonium phosphate, potassium nitrate, etc.). The numbers 8-10-8 denote the percentages of nitrogen, phosphorous, and potassium present in this mix. This example contains 8 percent nitrogen, 10 percent phosphorous, and 8 percent potassium. Some fertilizers also contain secondary and micro-nutrients. Look for fertilizers with micro-nutrients derived from EDTA complexes as they are water soluble and hence immediately available to the root system. Rose foods containing all three levels of nutrients (primary, secondary, and micro-) are the best choice. In some cases, a soil penetrant will be added to the fertilizer to assist in delivery of the nutrients in clay soils.

FERTILIZERS

ORGANIC
Alfalfa meal
Bone meal
Cottonseed meal
Dried blood
Fish scrap
Guanos, manures
Humus
Peat
Milorganite

INORGANIC
Ammonium
   phosphate
Ammonium Sulfate
Calcium nitrate
Magnesium sulfate
Potassium phosphates
Potassium chloride
Potassium nitrate
Sodium nitrate
Sulfate of potash
   magnesia

and foliar liquids are sprayed on and absorbed by the leaves. Whatever you use, be sure to follow the directions and dosages exactly. Excessive doses can damage plants.

Most roses need regular feeding—with fertilizers that are balanced for roses, your region, and your garden soil. Begin fertilizing newly planted roses once they are established—about three to four weeks after planting. Start feeding older plants in spring when new growth is about 6 inches long. At a minimum, species roses, old roses, and climbers need an application in the early spring as the buds prepare to open. Repeat-blooming roses, old roses, and climbers will benefit from a second

feeding of liquid fertilizer after the first bloom, and modern roses need regular feeding.

Alfalfa pellets worked into the soil are an organic source of nitrogen and can be used as a slow-release supplement in spring. Use pellets that are not feed-grade so your rose food doesn't feed the rabbits. A time-release synthetic fertilizer applied in the spring and again in July will reduce the need for reapplications. In zone 6 and colder, stop fertilizing six weeks before the average date of the first frost and let plants harden off for their winter rest.

REGULAR FEEDING SCHEDULE

Roses are heavy feeders. They require a constant supply of nutrients to sustain growth and bloom production. Here are two methods that will meet their demand for food:

■ **The Organic Method:** Regularly-spaced applications of fertilizers dispersed on the rose beds about every four weeks for a continuing cycle of decomposition to supply sufficient nutrients. It is best to work the fertilizer into the upper soil levels. This program can be supplemented with biweekly applications of fish emulsion.

■ **The Chemical-Fertilizer Method:** Start with a time-release synthetic in the spring and reapply midsummer, with monthly applications of a complete rose food (with all primary, secondary, and micro-nutrients) in between major feedings. Always follow label application and safety instructions when using a chemical rose food.

FERTILIZING CONTAINERS

The increased watering required for container roses also leaches nutrients from the soil more quickly, and you will have to fertilize more often to make up for the loss. With both liquid and dry fertilizers, apply half as much twice as often (half strength of a water-soluble fertilizer, for example, every two weeks) but don't over-fertilize. If you mistakenly overdo it, soak the plant thoroughly to wash out the excess.

Solving Nutrient Problems

MATURE LEAF SETS AFFECTED

Use these diagnostic tables to identify common plant nutrition problems. If symptoms are localized to mostly mature leaf sets (those on stems already carrying blooms), use this page. If mostly emerging foliage is affected, consult the facing page. Shown at left is a healthy mature leaf set, with typically dark green leaflets.

SYMPTOMS OVER WHOLE BUSH

Nitrogen Deficiency:
Leaves lighter green to yellow, with random leaf spots. If soil is too acidic (pH 5.8 or less), apply lime (¼ to ½ cup per bush). If pH is OK, fertilize with high nitrogen fertilizer (1 to 2 tablespoons per bush).

Phosphorus Deficiency:
Leaves dark green developing dark red and purple colors, mainly within leaf (colors can also spread to outer edges). If soil is too acidic, apply lime. If pH is OK, fertilize with high phosphorous fertilizer (20%), 1 to 2 tablespoons per bush.

LOCALIZED SYMPTOMS IN SMALLER AREAS

Potassium Deficiency:
Dead tissue, mainly at edges of leaves. If soil is too acidic, apply lime. If soil pH is OK, feed weekly with 2 tablespoons (for hybrid teas) of ammonium nitrate.

Zinc Deficiency:
Large areas of dead tissue at tips and between veins. Apply lime to correct pH. If pH is OK, then apply zinc chelate (1 teaspoon per bush).

Magnesium Deficiency:
Yellowing starting from center of leaf, with signs of dying tissue overlaying the affected parts. Apply Epsom salts, ½ cup sprinkled around the base of each bush.

EMERGING FOLIAGE AFFECTED

If symptoms are localized to emerging foliage, use this page the cause and treatment of the problem. Shown at left is an example of healthy emerging foliage, with normally purplish leaves on stems that do not yet have mature blooms.

TERMINAL BUD DEAD

Calcium Deficiency:
Young leaves are hooked. Apply calcium nitrate (1 to 2 tablespoons per bush per week) until corrected.

Boron Deficiency:
Young leaves are light green at base and twisted. Apply 1 teaspoon Borax per bush.

Copper Deficiency:
Young leaves are permanently wilted with no chlorosis (yellowing). Apply copper sulfate (¼ teaspoon per bush).

TERMINAL BUD ALIVE

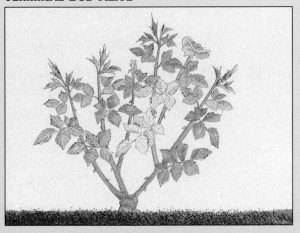

Sulfur Deficiency:
Leaves are light green with lighter-green veins. Apply soil sulfur (2 tablespoons per bush) or apply a fertilizer containing this element.

Iron Deficiency:
Leaves are yellow with principal veins light green. Use iron chelate (¼ teaspoon per bush) for immediate correction. Iron sulfate takes longer to act.

Watering

Water is vital in delivering nutrients to the plant. It travels up the canes (depositing nutrients for new stem and flower growth), and down (to build a stronger network of roots).

The circulatory system of the rose is not immune from challenges. Chief among them is the loss of water from pores in the leaves. This process is called transpiration, and when under-watered roots can't keep up with the watering needs of the plant, it wilts. Overwatering, on the other hand, starves the roots of oxygen, and the lower leaves turn yellow and fall off. Normally, you should give your roses 1 to 2 inches of water each week—in single watering session—from early spring through fall. Increase the frequency to every three or four days in hot and dry weather. Porous soils will also benefit from additional deep soakings.

Soak the soil to a 16- to 18-inch depth; light sprinkling does more harm than not watering at all, because the roots will not grow deeply enough to support the plant. Lightly watered plants are more easily injured by cultivation and they are also more prone to fertilizer burn.

An underwatered plant: Its stems and foliage tend to droop and sag.

Water to Penetrate Roots: *Roses have large root systems and efficient watering must provide a relatively quick and even distribution of water throughout all the roots. A watering wand is a good way to get water to the roots.*

WATER ROSES WELL

Check the depth of your watering to make sure it's reaching the roots. Water for a measured length of time and dig near the roots. If the soil is moist to a level of only 8 inches, you should water twice as long.

There are several options when it comes to choosing the method of applying water. Your choice will depend on your location, the size of your garden, the need for water conservation, and other factors. Among your choices are drip irrigation, underground sprinklers, or hand watering. Drip or low-volume irrigation is an efficient method that releases water to your plant without runoff. You can place an emitter on each side of your rose, use manufactured drip collars, or fashion your own with perforated drip tubing.

Conventional spray heads direct water up onto the foliage, removing spider mites, which live on the underside of the leaves. Low volume mini-sprays apply water more economically, but don't do as good a job in wetting the foliage.

Plants that are overwatered are starved of oxygen; their lower foliage sets turn yellow and fall off.

If you're hand watering, you may want to consider using a bubbler attachment. By flooding a basin around the rose, it allows water to soak slowly into the soil, and prevents a strong stream from eroding the soil or splashing dirt and mulch up onto the foliage. (Bubbler heads attached to underground systems accomplish this task even more conveniently.) Apply a 2- to 4-inch layer of mulch on top of the soil in order to slow the evaporation of water from the soil. Mulching also insulates the ground in winter so it freezes and thaws gradually, which prevents plants from "heaving."

ROSES IN CONTAINERS

Roses grown in containers need more attention than those grown directly in the garden because they have less soil from which to draw moisture.

Check the moisture depth in the pot at least every one or two days during the summer—every day when the weather is hot or windy. Unglazed pots lose moisture to the air more quickly than those made of plastic or glazed pottery. You can also put one container inside another to reduce moisture loss, but be sure the outside container has drainage holes, too.

How to Cut a Hybrid Tea:
When removing a blossom or a spent bloom always cut just above a five-leaflet set with a thickness that will support the successive stem.

How to Groom a Grandiflora or a Floribunda Spray:
To achieve maximum flower effect in a spray or open cluster, disbud the central bud after it appears. The remaining florets in the spray will all bloom at the same time. After it has finished blooming, cut the spray to the nearest five-leaflet set that will support the next stem to sprout.

Grooming, Weeding, And Cleaning

Roses are not plants that thrive on neglect. They love attention and care. With regular grooming, weeding, and a little picking up after them, your roses will not only resist disease and insects, they will reward you season after season.

After the first and second bloom cycles, begin removing blossoms that are spent. This process, called deadheading, allows the plant to channel its energy into producing more blooms instead of seed. Deadheaded plants will rebloom more quickly, are likely to grow stronger stems, and generally look more attractive. Cut the spent blossom back to the nearest five leaflets where the stem is about as thick as a pencil. Make sure the swollen eye (on which the new flower stem will grow) points to the outside of the bush. Leave as much foliage on the bush as possible. After deadheading, the leaflet at the cut may turn yellow and fall off. Don't worry, this is normal.

HOW TO DISBUD ROSES

If you're growing grandifloras and floribundas, a practice called disbudding can produce spectacular results. These roses normally bloom in clusters; the central flower blooms first, followed by the secondary buds. The central flower inhibits the development of the lower side buds. Remove it and the surrounding buds burst into a larger display.

The summer months are an ideal time to open up the central area of each bush to improve air circulation and suppress fungal diseases. Remove twiggy growth not capable of supporting new growth. Cut off such weak growth all the way back to the main cane or stem. While this loss of foliage surface is not always desirable, the benefits from removal are worthwhile. It is also an ideal opportunity to remove any dead wood or dying stems.

Remove weeds at the first sign of growth; once they become established they're stubborn. Suppress them with landscape fabrics and/or mulch and pull those that do appear before they get a foothold. Should the dreaded weed oxalis persist, a herbicide may be necessary. However, exercise extreme caution using herbicides. If the spray drifts onto rose foliage, it might cause dwarfed and wrinkled foliage or even kill the plant. In particular, remove dead foliage and other leaf litter from the beds. This debris is a home for pests and fungal spores that could plague the rose bush later in the summer.

HOW TO MULCH ROSES

Besides helping to retain moisture, mulching is also an effective weed control and reduces the need for cultivation, which, if done too deeply (more than 1 to 1½ inches), can damage feeder roots. You can apply mulch to single plants or over a whole bed. Organic mulches, such as bark, grass clippings, rotted manure, straw, and shredded leaves, break down and improve the soil. Landscape fabric blocks light that weeds need for germination, but lets water through. Mulch after planting—2 to 4 inches, but don't mound it around the base of the plants. If you experience problems with fungal diseases, remove the mulch in the fall each year. In cold winter regions, wait until the soil warms to replace it.

GOOD MULCH

Redwood (small bark)
Mushroom compost
Rotted manures
Straw
Shredded tree leaves
Pine needles
Aged sawdust
Home compost
Pine straw
Cocoa bean shells
Rice hulls
Ground corn cobs

Protection from Pests and Diseases

For many gardeners new to rose-growing, trying to grow healthy, pest-free roses is a major concern, even a deterrent to getting started. Although some roses are particularly prone to infestation, a look at the history of roses will show you what survivors these flowering shrubs are, flourishing in abandoned yards and cemeteries with little to no care. It's plain to see that most pests are obstacles that can be overcome without hours of back-breaking effort. At the same time, it's also clear what roses are capable of when we provide them with prime growing conditions. After all, the rose is a hardy, adaptable family of plants. How we perceive the pest problem is more than half the battle toward solving it.

Good bugs for the garden: Both the easily identifiable adult ladybug (or lady beetle) and its less familiar, slate-gray larvae eat great quantities of aphids. They cannot be lured by specific plants but will be encouraged into the garden by growing a varied selection of plants.

APPROACHES TO PEST MANAGEMENT

As we proceed into a new millenium, a more environmentally enlightened age is upon us. Many home gardeners have come to prefer addressing pest management with naturally based products, and then only when they detect a problem that has not been resolved by the natural balance of the garden. This "organic" approach to gardening does require, however, a certain tolerance of low-level pest damage from time to time. "Eat and let eat," one famous garden designer advises. Many gardeners who grow roses are relaxed enough to be quite satisfied with the level of success provided by organic gardening.

At the other extreme, traditional rose gardening—primarily driven by the need to grow perfect, exhibition-quality hybrid tea blooms—has long been connected with the intensive use of chemical sprays to prevent even the hint of pest and disease damage. In general, if you want roses consistently perfect in every way, you will need to use chemicals.

Before deciding on your approach, identify your goals and needs. How unblemished do you need your roses to be? How many aphids on your prize blooms can you live with? Is a small amount of mildew acceptable? Are you planning on competing for trophies, or are you just interested in a few blooms for the table? Is perfection a realistic goal?

INTEGRATED PEST MANAGEMENT

Of all approaches available today for controlling rose-related pests and diseases, Integrated Pest Management (IPM) is a balanced approach that makes the most sense for the home gardener. Integrated Pest Management rests on three principles: First,

have clear goals and know the level of damage you are willing to tolerate; second, treat the pest, not the garden, targeting specific problems you have observed before they become overwhelming; and third, use natural controls first, low-toxicity chemicals only if natural controls fail, and extreme measures only as a last resort.

Integrated Pest Management can be thought of as a pyramid with five levels from a broad foundation to a narrow, precise top:

1. Plant selection and good gardening;
2. Close observation and inspection;
3. Natural and non-chemical intervention;
4. Low-toxicity chemical intervention; and
5. Extreme chemical intervention.

1. PROPER PLANT SELECTION AND GOOD GARDENING

The first key to growing healthy roses is to select varieties known to be healthy-growing roses for your area. The Rose Selection Guide on pages 50 through 91 of this book will help you identify varieties that have been bred to be especially pest- and disease-resistant. Visit public rose gardens in your area, as well as the rose gardens of friends and neighbors, and note the varieties that look the healthiest. Consult with local rosarians affiliated with the American Rose Society (find out how on page 92). Ask for recommendations at your local nursery or garden center.

The second key to growing healthy roses is simple, basic horticultural practice. Plan the garden so that the roses receive at least six to eight hours of sun a day. The more sun the better. Then plant your roses so that they do not crowd one another, providing optimum air circulation around and through the shrubs. This will lessen stagnant pockets that become an ideal home for disease and insects while also making it easier to keep weeds down. Pay attention to the basic horticultural needs of your roses, making sure they are receiving sufficient water, either from rain or irrigation.

As we try to avoid stress in our own lives, so roses thrive best when hardship is avoided. Lack of sufficient water or nutrition can create such hardship and open pathways for infestation. Feed roses with a balanced fertilizer on a regular schedule, making sure not to apply too much nitrogen. When overused, this essential fertilizer component causes succulent growth (which is more attractive to insects and more susceptible to disease). Balance is the key. Use enough nitrogen to encourage growth and bloom, and not so much as to foster problems.

2. OBSERVATION

Survey the level of trouble in your garden while performing your regular chores. Identify problems before they become overwhelming. Check for insects and disease as you prune or water. Use the illustrations and list on pages 40 and 41 to help you identify common rose problems. If a particular rose isn't strong and is prone to attack to the point of hardship, remove it. Plant a more vigorous bush in its place. Be aware that many rose pests and diseases are strongly effected by climate and season. For example, powdery mildew tends to be the most serious when the days are warm and humid and nights cool. In many areas, aphids are not a concern when the weather is hot and dry. These conditions are predictable, so in regions with less than optimal weather conditions, you can learn to take precautions *before* you notice damage resulting from an outbreak.

3. NATURAL INTERVENTION

If a problem arises, turn first to natural and non-chemical intervention. Use water to knock off aphids, or rinse off the underside of rose foliage to remove mites. Clean foliage is healthy foliage. A few products that use biocompatible fungicidal components such as sodium and potassium bicarbonates are on or coming onto the market. These products are proving to be effective in controlling the major foliar diseases in the rose family.

A good response can be to release predatory insects into your garden to help get pests under control. Remember that there is a difference between control and annihilation. This is the line many thoughtful gardeners are choosing as their final level of intervention, making a conscious decision not to use anything stronger.

4. LOW-TOXICITY INTERVENTION

In some circumstances, it will be necessary to proceed to more serious intercession. Just above nature's own tools on the pyramid, Level 4 includes a number of low-toxicity interventions that are currently available. It may be necessary at times to resort to these slightly more toxic solutions in order to properly address a more implacable foe. Products such as horticultural soap that are modified to control insects or diseases are short-term solutions to these problems. Horticultural oils, used when the weather permits (temperatures must not be higher than 80°F, or foliage damage will occur), are quite effective against some of the more stubborn pests and diseases.

5. EXTREME INTERVENTION

For some gardeners, extreme chemical intervention is a perfectly acceptable last resort. But there are wiser choices even here. Products such as neem oil or pyrethrins are effective short-term insecticides and can be used with relative safety. They will kill insect allies, however, so don't use them if you have gone to the expense of releasing predatory insects, such as lady bugs.

The apex of the pyramid is the extreme of using even more drastic chemicals. This is the level that, today, causes many of us the greatest alarm. Experience teaches us that caution is warranted. Read the labels! Follow the instructions to the letter! And only resort to chemical intervention on a selective basis. Treat the problem, not the garden. If one bush has an infestation of spider mites, then spray only that affected plant.

For many gardeners today, chemical intervention is simply not an option, and less-than-perfect roses are quite acceptable. For other rose enthusiasts, a steady application of chemicals is the only way to achieve the perfection they desire. Integrated Pest Management offers a balanced road down the middle. Ultimately, the choice is yours.

HOW TO SELECT A SPRAYER

The choice of sprayers available to rose growers is dependent on the size of the garden. The following is a guide to help you select an appropriate and durable sprayer with the proper capacity for your garden:
SMALL GARDEN (UP TO 10 PLANTS): The best choice here is a quart-sprayer. Such devices provide a handy 1-quart compression sprayer with a high-pressure plastic tank. Units usually have a unique on/off or continuous-on trigger design. The nozzle adjusts spray from a fine mist to a 30-foot jet stream for those hard-to-reach climbers and ramblers.
MEDIUM GARDEN (10 TO 30 PLANTS): The choice here is for at least a 1-gallon sprayer. It only takes a single pump to spray the entire 1 gallon. Units are made of tough, high-impact injection-molded plastic, with a pressure-control gauge for low pressure and no-drift spraying. Comes with 20-inch wand.
LARGE GARDEN (30 TO 100 PLANTS): With this larger garden it is wise to invest in a backpack-sprayer unit with a capacity of 4 gallons (it delivers 75 pounds working pressure per square inch).
VERY LARGE GARDEN (100 TO 500 PLANTS): For mobility, the best choice is a cordless electric sprayer that uses a 12-volt rechargeable battery with a 6-gallon plastic tank and 10 to 20 feet of hose (it delivers 60 pounds working pressure per square inch). Recharging time is approximately eight hours.

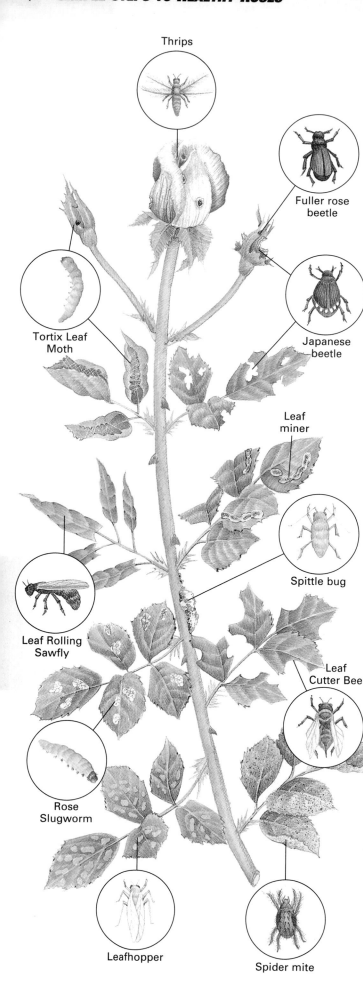

Thrips

Fuller rose beetle

Japanese beetle

Tortix Leaf Moth

Leaf miner

Spittle bug

Leaf Rolling Sawfly

Leaf Cutter Bee

Rose Slugworm

Leafhopper

Spider mite

Identifying and Controlling Garden Pests

There are three main categories of pests to watch out for—various insects, spider mites, and fungal diseases. This section deals mainly with a visual identification scheme and some suggestions for control.

THRIP: The adult thrip is about $\frac{1}{16}$ inch long, and usually has a dark body with four fringed wings. Its small size makes this pest often difficult to detect in the garden. It mainly attacks tender young leaf tissue, flower stalks, and flower buds. Spraying with a suitable insecticide should be directed at young tender foliage and developing buds as well as the soil around the bush.

JAPANESE BEETLE, FULLER ROSE BEETLE: These are two beetles that will indiscriminately eat parts of the foliage, sometimes the flower parts. While beetles can be picked off the bush by hand, their larvae are subterranean dwellers that can be disposed of with a soil drench of an appropriate insecticide.

TORTIX LEAF MOTH: This insect lays eggs on the underside of foliage and rolls the leaf into a protective cover, using a silken thread to hold the foliage in a cocoon-like structure. This allows the developing caterpillar to feed. Remove and destroy foliage.

LEAF MINER: This insect is easily spotted on the foliage by the appearance of irregular white chain-like blisters containing its grub. Foliage should be removed and discarded to prevent further infection.

LEAF ROLLING SAWFLY: This fly lays its eggs in the leaf margins with the leaf rolling up into a strange looking cocoon-like structure. At this stage it is best to remove the leaf and destroy the grubs inside; otherwise the colony will quickly spread.

SPITTLE BUG: This small, greenish-yellow insect always hides inside a circular mass of white foam on the surface of new stems, usually during the development of the first bloom cycle in early spring. A strong jet spray of water will remove the foam and the insect.

ROSE SLUGWORM: When you detect new foliage with a skeletonized pattern indicating the foliage has been eaten (but not the vein structure), then chances are the rose slugworm has been at work. It is best to remove the infected foliage or spray regularly with an insecticide.

LEAF CUTTER BEE: Regarded as a beneficial insect, the leaf cutter carves out semicircular portions of foliage as nest tunnels and fodder for its young. Live with the damage, for this insect is a natural predator for other pests.

LEAFHOPPER: As its name implies, this very small yellowish-green insect jumps on the undersides of foliage to feast, often leaving its white skin behind. The damage caused by this insect can often result in defoliation. Use of an insecticide will prevent it from establishing a strong colony.

SPIDER MITE: The spider mite establishes huge colonies underneath leaves, giving the appearance of salt-and-pepper particles. If detected early enough, the problem can be controlled chemically with another group of pesticides called miticides or acaricides.

Spraying with such products, however, demands that the spray be directed to the underside of the leaves to target the colonies for direct attack. If you prefer, a fine misting with water to the undersides of the foliage will wash off the mites to ground level, and since they are unable to fly they will die on the surface.

ROSE APHID: Number one insect enemy in the rose garden is undoubtedly the aphid (often referred to as greenfly). The rose aphid is a small, green, soft-bodied insect (about 1/16 inch long) that can be found in large colonies, particularly on the first lush spring growth, sucking the sap from the stems via puncture holes. For control, they can be washed off the stems with water or sprayed with an insecticide.

CAPSID BUG: This insect is easily spotted on the buds as it is usually bright green. It feeds on buds and foliage, resulting in distortion or wilting. An application of an insecticide will solve the problem.

POWDERY MILDEW: This fungus feeds on roses by imbedding its own living structure into the cellular layer just below the epidermis. It then feeds on the sap, extending its structure on the surface. Control using a fungicide. The waxy coating of some rose leaves provides a good barrier to the fungus.

DOWNY MILDEW: Perhaps the most serious fungus to invade the rose garden is downy mildew, a big brother to powdery mildew. It can defoliate a rose bush and continue to survive on the canes themselves. Control preventively with a fungicide. Practice good sanitation; pick up fallen leaves and prunings and dispose of them in the trash.

BLACKSPOT: This fungus causes circular black spots on the surface of leaves. It tends to thrive in warm, wet climates with high humidity. Control with a fungicide. Practice good sanitation; pick up fallen leaves and place in trash; do not compost them.

ROSE SCALE: This insect hides under gray scales or shells normally on old canes or stems. It feeds by sucking the sap and hence weakens the plant. If localized, it can often be removed with your fingernail or spraying with an insecticide.

RUST: This is another fungus that can invade the garden, especially when moisture levels are high. It grows on the undersides of the foliage in little red clusters. Rust is destroyed by an application of a suitable fungicide.

VIRUS: Two viral infections sometimes attack roses, appearing as yellow or cream veining that gives the foliage a variegated look. Vein banding mosaic is not a serious problem. Line pattern rose mosaic, however, can weaken the plant and cause death. Remove and destroy plants with either of these two infections to avoid spread in the garden.

CANE BORER: This insect is the maggot of the eggs laid by sawflies or carpenter bees deep in the freshly cut cane of the rose after pruning. The telltale sign of a cane borer is the neatly punctured hole visible on the top of the cane. To remove the pest, cut several inches down the cane until there are no longer signs of the maggot or pith-eaten core.

Rose aphid

Capsid bug

Powdery mildew

Downy mildew

Blackspot

Rust

Rose scale

Vein banding rose mosaic

Cane borer

Line pattern rose mosaic

Protection from the Elements

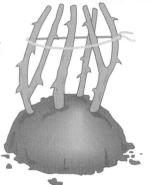

ROSES HARDY TO ZONE 4

HYBRID TEAS
'Brigadoon', 'Elina', 'Folklore', 'Fragrant Cloud', 'Ingrid Bergman', 'Kardinal', 'Lynn Anderson', 'Midas Touch', and 'Timeless'

FLORIBUNDAS
'Betty Prior', 'Cherish', 'French Lace', 'Iceberg', 'Lavaglut', 'Little Darling', 'Permanent Wave', 'Playboy', 'Scentimental', and 'Sexy Rexy'

OLD GARDEN ROSES
'Apothecary's Rose', 'Austrian Copper', 'Cardinal de Richelieu', 'Charles de Mills', 'Enfant de France', 'Ferdinand Pichard', 'Konigin von Danemark', 'La Belle Sultane', 'Rose de Meaux', 'Salet', and 'Superb Tuscan'

SHRUBS
Most of the classic and modern shrubs in the Rose Selection Guide (pages 72 to 87) are hardy to zone 4. The following are hardy to zone 3: 'Blanc Double de Coubert', 'Carefree Wonder', 'Frau Dagmar Hartopp', 'Hansa', Rosa rugosa, 'Therese Bugnet'

MINIATURES
'Behold', 'Glowing Amber', 'Gourmet Popcorn', 'Green Ice', 'Little Artist', 'Minnie Pearl', 'Old Glory', and 'Roller Coaster'

CLIMBING ROSES
'Colette', 'Constance Spry', 'Dortmund', 'Dublin Bay', 'Eden', 'Jeanne LaJoie', 'Joseph's Coat', 'Lavender Lassie', 'New Dawn', 'Paul's Himalayan Musk', 'Polka', 'Prosperity', 'Sally Holmes', and 'William Baffin'

WINTER PROTECTION

The first maxim of winter protection is this: If you select plants that are hardy to winter in your area, you won't have to worry that much about protecting them. One of the most important aspects of selection is to buy roses budded onto rootstock that will survive your climate—for example, multiflora for zone 6 and colder—and to plant the bud union at the correct level for your zone.

HARDY BY NATURE

Hardiness is a measure of the ability of a rose to survive winter temperatures. (For further discussion, see "Roses and Your Climate," page 53.) Many species roses, shrubs, old roses, and climbers, as well as some of the newer hybrid teas and floribundas, survive freezing and need little or no protection. Miniatures are more cold resistant than hybrid teas, and need little protection (in zones 6 and warmer, only 12 inches of dried leaves).

How much protection you provide is therefore governed by the severity of your winter cold and the

Rose-Cone Protection: *Trim, defoliate, and mound up the bush with about 12 to 24 inches of soil and mulch. Tie up canes, place protective cone, and weigh it down. After last frost, uncover to reveal dieback, which should be pruned off.*

hardiness of the rose you have selected. In areas where it rarely freezes, no winter protection is necessary. In any area where freezing is common, you'll need to protect roses that you're stretching out of their zone.

Sometimes nature will do it for you. That first thick blanket of snow can be a good insulation *if it stays in place for some time*. It keeps temperatures beneath it from dipping too far below freezing, but low enough to keep the plant in dormancy. Snow layers can also

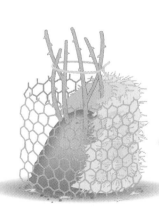

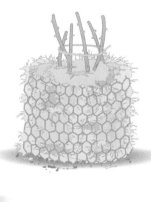

How to Protect a Rose Bush: *Using a collar of chicken wire, mound the rose bush with soil and mulch. Next, fill in the space between the canes with leaves, straw, and mulch. Any canes* protruding from the chicken wire collar may die back and can be removed during pruning. Remember, this is not necessary for areas in southern zone 8 and higher.

keep the canes from drying out in the wind. Unfortunately, not everyone lives where snow provides a dependable cover all winter.

PROVIDING EXTRA PROTECTION

Many gardeners are unable to resist growing plants not rated to be hardy in their area. If you are one of those adventurers, you will need to provide special winter protection for your roses. In a cylinder made from chicken wire, cover the roses with about 12 inches of soil and an additional 12 inches of leaves (shredded oak leaves work well). This will protect the bud union and the lower portion of the canes. Remove the mound in spring and work it into the soil. You can also use rose cones made of polystyrene or compressed fiber. They're sold at garden centers in several sizes and should be filled with mounded soil and mulch. Weight them down with a brick and when the weather warms, remove the top (or cut the top off) to allow air circulation and to inhibit the growth of mold and fungi.

If you're growing climbers, untie them from their support, tie them together in a bundle, and wrap them in burlap. To get tree roses through severe winters, partially dig them up, lay them on their side, and cover them with a mixture of soil and mulch.

When temperatures fall below 28° F, it's time to relocate your roses in containers. Move them to an unheated shelter or garage (but not colder than 10° F), away from the wind. When the foliage begins to fall, remove the remaining leaves completely. Water the plants occasionally but do not fertilize them. When all danger of spring frost is past, move the roses in their containers back outside. Prune them lightly to start new growth.

In areas where the temperature stays above 28° F (zones 9 and 10), your roses in containers can stay outside all winter long. Remember to cut back on their water and do not fertilize them while they're dormant.

SUN-PROOF AND RAIN-PROOF VARIETIES

Besides protection from cold, several rose varieties are known for their stamina against strong sunlight and frequent rain showers. Some of the best are:

HYBRID TEAS:
'Brandy'
'Crystalline'
'Gold Medal'
'Ingrid Bergman'
'Perfect Moment'
'Signature'
'Touch of Class'

FLORIBUNDAS:
'Amber Queen'
'Blueberry Hill'
'Dicky'
'Gene Boerner'
'Iceberg'
'Nicole'
'Playboy'

MINIATURES:
'Behold'
'Carrot Top'
'Gourmet Popcorn'
'Miss Flippins'
'Old Glory'
'Starina'

ROSES MORE TOLERANT OF SHADE

Best roses for areas of the garden with less than six hours of sun per day.

FLORIBUNDAS:
'Betty Boop'
'Blueberry Hill'
'Ivory Fashion'
'Playboy'
'Playgirl'
'Sweet Vivian'

MINIATURES:
'Green Ice'
'Pinstripe'
'Roller Coaster'
'Sweet Chariot'

SHRUBS:
'Carefree Beauty'
'Carefree Delight'
'Carefree Wonder'
'Erfurt'
'Flutterbye'
'Gruss an Aachen'

How to Protect a Climber: Trim, defoliate, and tie canes up into a neat vertical bundle. Wrap the bundle with burlap, canvas, or a similar fabric (never plastic), and tie down for security. Mound up the base of the plant with a mixture of mulch and soil.

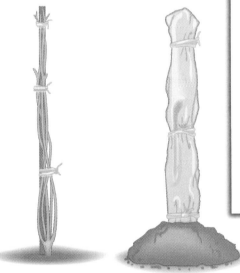

How to Protect Standard Tree Roses: *Trim and defoliate the bush and partially uncover the root system to allow the tree to lay on its side. Hold the entire plant in place with crossed stakes, and cover it with a mixture of soil and mulch.*

Pruning

Pruning Basics

Of all gardening chores, pruning seems to create the most anxiety. It need not be that way. Like any skill, you can learn the rudiments from books and demonstrations, but it's your own hands-on experience that will translate that information into working knowledge. If you make a few mistakes along the way, it won't result in disaster; your rose will still perform. And as you get to know your roses, proper pruning will enhance your enjoyment and pride in helping nature present its best. Approach pruning like an artist—after all, you're about to create a masterpiece. Try to imagine what the bush will look like. Let your inspiration flow.

Pruning gives you an annual opportunity to correct, adjust, and modify the growth of your roses to increase their flower production. Pruning times and techniques will vary somewhat with the types of roses in your garden and where you live. (See page 48 for a discussion of pruning practices for each variety.) But in all cases it enhances the architecture of the plant, ensures a vigorous first bloom, and encourages new growth from the bud union. Removing old and damaged wood allows the plant to recuperate, and in warmer climates pruning is necessary to induce a kind of dormancy that cold-weather plants receive in winter. Even roses need a rest. During this period, plant growth is slowed and redirected toward producing those first magnificent blooms.

When and how much should you prune? Here are some rules of thumb. In general, you will be pruning just before the plant breaks dormancy after spring's final frost. This will be early in the year in warm climates, and anytime between January and April in cold climates. If it's old roses you are tending, prune them after blooming. They bear flowers on last year's wood. Cut away the dead wood first—it will help you "see" the shape of the plant without distraction.

It's a good idea to visit a public rose garden and find specimens of roses you are growing. Note how the gardeners have pruned roses of the same type. In cold winter climates, pruning is often reduced to one option: simply cut back the wood that was killed in winter. In warm climates, pruning can be done at any of three levels, depending on your purpose. Severe pruning (cut to leave three or four canes, 6 to 10 inches high) produces fewer but larger blooms. Moderate pruning (five to 12 canes cut to 18 to 24 inches) makes for a larger bush. And light pruning (less than one-third of the plant is thinned out) increases the number of short-stemmed flowers that will be produced.

WHAT TOOLS YOU WILL NEED

Invest in a pair of high-quality pruning shears with both blades curved. (Those with a flat "anvil" on one blade tend to crush stems, not cut them.) This is one tool where price really does make a difference. Select a manufacturer with a proven track record, and buy the best that you can afford. Some pruning shears

Basic pruning tools include leather gauntlet gloves, curved blade pruning shears for typical cane thicknesses (buy one with a swivel handle to reduce wrist strain), small pruning shears for smaller rose and miniatures, long-handled loppers for heavy canes, and a pruning saw for cutting woody canes and dead wood.

Why prune?
By fall, miniature roses have grown tall and leggy. Colder evenings produce ill-formed, mottled blossoms and yellowing foliage that often starts to fall off (right). Rose hips, which can interrupt the next blooming cycle, may result if spent blossoms are not removed. Pruning removes diseased and dead stems and canes and reduces the overall size of the plant (below right). The first spring bloom demonstrates how pruning results in an annual process of renewal (below left).

Miniature plant as it looks in the late fall.

have a special hand grip designed for left-handed people. Others have swivel handles that are easier on your wrists, and there are models with removable blades for storage. Smaller versions (costing about $20) are available for pruning miniature roses. Next, you'll need a pruning saw to remove large woody canes. It will give you a clean cut without damage to the bud union. The third tool you need is a pair of lopping shears. Loppers are pruning shears with long (12- to 18-inch) handles. They will provide you with leverage for the thicker canes. Finally, buy a good strong pair of leather gauntlet gloves or hand gloves that are puncture-proof. Now, you're ready to start pruning.

After pruning in late winter.

The first spring bloom.

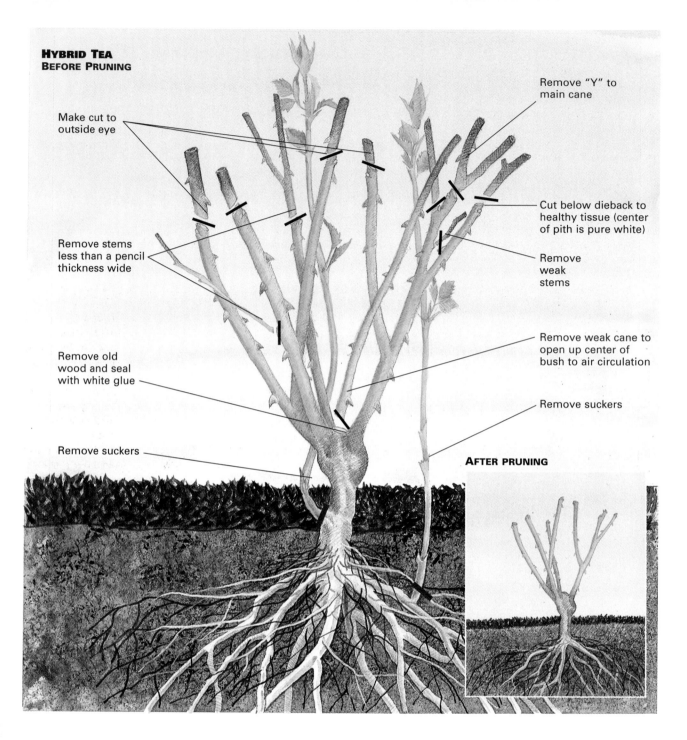

HYBRID TEA
BEFORE PRUNING

Make cut to outside eye

Remove "Y" to main cane

Remove stems less than a pencil thickness wide

Cut below dieback to healthy tissue (center of pith is pure white)

Remove weak stems

Remove old wood and seal with white glue

Remove weak cane to open up center of bush to air circulation

Remove suckers

Remove suckers

AFTER PRUNING

General Tips For Proper Pruning

1. Always prune dead wood back to healthy tissue. You will recognize the living tissue by its green bark and white pith core.
2. After you make each cut, cover it with a drop of white glue to ensure quick recovery, as well as provide protection against cane borers.
3. Prune to ensure the center of the bush is open for maximum air circulation.
4. Remove all growth on the main canes that is not capable of sustaining a reasonably thick stem on its own.
5. If suckers—growths from the root structure that sprout from below the bud union—are present, remove them as close to the main root cane as possible.
6. Remove woody old canes; saw them off as close to the bud union as you can get.
7. After you have completed pruning your rose bush, remove any remaining foliage from the canes and clean up debris from around the bush. Discard all foliage (do not use it in the compost heap).

Good Cuts, Bad Cuts

By far the most important rose-pruning technique to master is the art of the correct angle. Make your pruning cuts at a 45° angle, about ¼ inch above a leaf axle with a dormant eye. Choose an eye on the outside of the cane and slope the cut down and away on the opposite side. This allows excess natural sap to rise and seal the cut without interfering with the developing eye. Pruning to an outward-facing bud also promotes outward growth, opens up the plant to air circulation, creates more pleasing shapes, resists disease, and prevents the canes from becoming a tangle. Cuts closer to the eye than ¼ inch may damage it. Cuts higher than that will leave a visible stubble— a haven for both pests and disease.

If the rose bush has foliage present, the location is easy to spot. Where there is no foliage to guide you, find the dormant eye by locating where the foliage was once connected. The eye is normally visible as a slight swelling above the surface of the cane.

Use this same pruning technique when cutting stems for display and when removing spent blooms. Remember to sharpen your pruning tools periodically—either do it yourself or have someone do it who's specially trained. Wipe metal surfaces after each use with a soft, lightly oiled rag to prevent rust. Store tools in a dry area. Master these simple rules and your spring rose growth will be guaranteed to produce a pleasing overall shape and habit for the rest of the season.

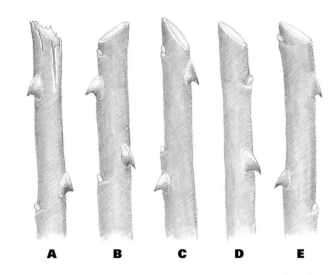

A   B   C   D   E

Find the Dormant Bud Eye (right): *Look for a slight swelling resembling a small pimple where the foliage has fallen off the cane. That's the dormant bud eye that will produce a new stem.*

Make the Right Cut (above): ***A:*** *Damaged cut caused by blunt blades on old pruners.* ***B:*** *Cut made at wrong angle.* ***C:*** *Angle too steep.* ***D:*** *Cut made too far above the bud eye.* ***E:*** *The proper cut for a rose cane.*

Why It's Important to Make the Correct Cut: *When the cut is made correctly— here, above an aging five-leaflet set with a dormant eye below (left)—* *the sap will rise from the rose cane and run down its opposite side (center). Remove the old leaf set just below the cut. Within a few weeks the dormant bud eye will begin to* *swell. In another three weeks the swelling will result in a young new stem (right) showing just a few foliage sets. Eventually that growth will become a stem and bloom.*

BEFORE PRUNING

AFTER PRUNING

How to Prune a Floribunda: Cut a little bit higher than for hybrid teas and leave as many canes as possible to produce lots and lots of sprays.

Pruning Roses in Mild Climates

Now that you're acquainted with the pruning basics, you're ready to apply them to your roses. The following instructions pertain to roses grown in mild-winter climates. The pruning differences for each variety don't apply to cold-winter gardeners because of the die-back caused by the cold. For cold-winter pruning instructions, see the box "Pruning in a Winter Climate" on this page.

HYBRID TEAS AND GRANDIFLORAS

By winter, hybrid tea roses and grandifloras are generally 8 to 10 feet tall and looking rather lanky. You can prune these canes (on an established bush) 2 to 4 feet but, in general, leave 4 to 5 major canes with an average height of 3 feet. Remove the older canes; it will trigger the rose bush to attempt basal breaks (new cane growth) in the spring. This regenerative process is fundamental to the health of the bush.

FLORIBUNDAS AND POLYANTHAS

Since floribundas and polyanthas are mainly for garden display rather than cut flowers, you can allow more older canes to remain for increased flower production. Cut back about one third of the year's new growth and leave substantially more stems than you would for a hybrid tea (see illustration, left). By nature, floribundas and polyanthas produce large numbers of flowers. Leaving a greater number of canes enhances the ability of the rose bush to produce the maximum number of flowers.

MINIATURE ROSES

Most miniature roses are grown on their own roots. There is no bud union and no suckers. Precise pruning of miniature roses is very labor intensive, and many rosarians simply use a hedge clipper to trim off the tops at a foot above the soil (height varies with the variety). After such treatment, remove any twiggy growth and open up the center of the plant to increase air circulation.

OLD GARDEN ROSES AND SHRUBS

When pruning old garden roses, don't treat them as modern hybrid teas or floribundas. For maximum blooms, pruning should be more of a light grooming than severe. Prune only last year's growth; prune

PRUNING IN A WINTER CLIMATE

In colder climates, most of this pruning advice still applies. Northerners just don't have as many height decisions to make. Where winter snow and freezing temperatures are commonplace, precise pruning for each variety is not necessary because—in spite of the winter protection measures we have taken—canes will die in the cold and must be cut back severely.

Remove all diseased and dead, blackened canes and then prune a little more off each remaining cane until you see center pith that is creamy-white, not brownish. Remove

any weak, twiggy growth and canes that cross each other and rub in the wind. Then stand back and admire what you have left and be glad your severe winter also killed most insects and fungal diseases. Two additional thoughts to keep in mind: Never prune in the fall, as it encourages new growth and even more winter kill; and, in spring, wait until all danger of severe weather is past before uncovering and pruning your roses. As the old saying goes, when the forsythia blooms, it is time to prune.

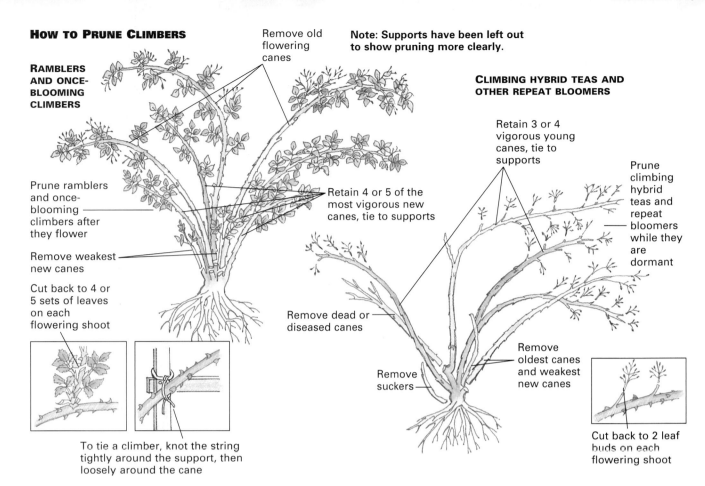

HOW TO PRUNE CLIMBERS

RAMBLERS AND ONCE-BLOOMING CLIMBERS

Remove old flowering canes

Note: Supports have been left out to show pruning more clearly.

CLIMBING HYBRID TEAS AND OTHER REPEAT BLOOMERS

Prune ramblers and once-blooming climbers after they flower

Remove weakest new canes

Cut back to 4 or 5 sets of leaves on each flowering shoot

Retain 4 or 5 of the most vigorous new canes, tie to supports

Retain 3 or 4 vigorous young canes, tie to supports

Prune climbing hybrid teas and repeat bloomers while they are dormant

Remove dead or diseased canes

Remove suckers

Remove oldest canes and weakest new canes

To tie a climber, knot the string tightly around the support, then loosely around the cane

Cut back to 2 leaf buds on each flowering shoot

one-time bloomers immediately after flowering; prune repeat bloomers in winter or early spring. After a few years, however, this practice makes for a very lanky bush, so each year thereafter prune back some of the oldest canes to promote basal and post-basal breaks. Keeping a proper balance between new growth and continuing old growth patterns is the secret to growing old garden roses.

CLIMBERS AND RAMBLERS

Climbers will generally not flower profusely unless the canes are trained on a horizontal plane. Cut the long-established canes to about the place where they are slightly thicker than a pencil. Then, cut each side stem that has flowered to the lowest possible five-leaflet stem, about 1 to 2 inches from the main cane. This process will cause the cane to flower along its complete length for a spectacular spring display.

AFTER PRUNING

Follow these suggestions in order to reduce the potential for disease as well as to encourage vigorous new growth:
1. Thoroughly clean the rose beds of dead leaves and other debris. You will reduce the potential for various insects and fungi to survive the winter by eliminating the places

in which they hide. Bag all pruned material from the bushes. Don't use rose stems for mulch or compost; many fungal spores can invade the stems and cause reinfections when the warmer weather returns.
2. To ensure the destruction of all insects and fungi, apply a dormant pesticide or fungicide spray immediately after pruning—when there are no eyes developing. Use the old-fashioned oil-and-sulfur spray to help destroy both powdery and downy mildew spores residing in the soil and on the canes. Inorganic sulfur compounds are available at garden centers. Follow instructions on the label to mix with horticultural oil.
3. After brushing the bud union with a wire brush to remove the old bark, cover the bud union with about 6 to 10 inches of the surrounding mulch. This protective mound of mulch keeps the bud union moist and receptive to new canes. Additionally, this mound can protect the bud union from mild frost and wind chill. Many rose experts avoid this step, believing it promotes a plant disease known as crown gall.
4. Avoid fertilization until about three or four weeks after pruning. Then apply 1 to 2 cups of a balanced granular rose food around the base of the mound covering the bud union, and then uncover the bud union. The mulch then provides a clean landscaping surface to start off the new year.

How to Prune a Climber: *Train the long canes into a horizontal position. Cut back flowering shoots, leaving four or five leaf sets. These small branches will produce next year's flowers. Canes older than 4 or 5 years should be removed to induce new growth.*

Rose
Selection Guide

Using this Guide

When you plant roses in your garden they will repay you with beauty and fragrance for many years to come. But which roses should you plant? The selections in this guide will help you answer that question. Here you will find described and illustrated over 350 roses from more than 20,000 cultivars currently available. They were chosen based on these factors: ease of availability coast to coast; vigor, disease resistance, and hardiness; fragrance, variety of color and shape; and ratings in nationwide evaluations. The selections are alphabetized within use categories that have been modified from the rose group classifications of the American Rose Society. "In This Chapter" at the lower corner of this page gives you a complete picture of these categories and where to find them.

Of course, any list will be, at least in part, subjective. The roses in this guide undeniably represent favorites. Never hesitate to experiment with other roses you find at nurseries and plant sales—there are literally thousands to learn about and enjoy.

READING THE SELECTION GUIDE

You'll find a number of abbreviations in the descriptions that accompany each entry. Here are some definitions:

RIR (ROSES IN REVIEW): This is a rating given to a rose after a three-year evaluation by growers from all regions of the country in the American Rose Society's Roses in Review program. The ratings translate as follows:

- 9.3–10.0: One of the best roses ever.
- 8.8–9.2: An outstanding rose.
- 8.3–8.7: A very good to excellent rose.
- 7.8–8.2: A solid to very good rose.
- 7.3–7.7: A good rose.
- 6.8–7.2: An average rose.
- 6.1–6.7: A below-average rose.
- 6.0 or less: Not recommended.

Not all roses have an RIR rating; some are too new to have completed their evaluation, and some older roses were not evaluated when the program began over 20 years ago.

Keep in mind that this rating is only an average of a number of characteristics important to gardeners, as well as an average of a variety's performance over the entire country. A rose may have a relatively low RIR rating, yet still be an outstanding performer in a more limited geographical area or possess desirable characteristics. If you are attracted to a low-rated rose, try it. It may perform surprisingly well in your garden.

AARS (ALL-AMERICA ROSE SELECTION): This denotes an award by commercial rose growers after a two-year standardized observation. Only three or four winners are designated annually from thousands of roses tested. This award, like the ratings of the RIR, is based on an average of performance throughout the country.

AOE (AWARD OF EXCELLENCE): This award for miniature roses is given by the American Rose Society after a two-year evaluation in six test gardens across the U.S.

ROSE HALL OF FAME: Every three years a ballot is taken for this prestigious award by the 32 member National Rose Societies belonging to the World Federation of Rose Societies. So far only nine roses have received this international status.

HARDINESS ZONES AND RECOMMENDED REGIONS. You will also find various abbreviations for geographic sections of the country that indicate areas within hardiness zones in which the selection will thrive. (See page 53.)

MAKING SELECTIONS

Each entry in the selection guide includes a color photograph, the cultivar name, year of introduction, awards (if applicable), unique characteristics, the geographic area in which the cultivar thrives (if applicable), petal count, the USDA hardiness zone, and Roses in Review (RIR) rating.

With this information, you can make selections that are specific to your garden and appealing to your tastes. If you're a beginning rose gardener, this guide will get you started—choose many or a few. But even if you're an experienced rose gardener, you'll find some exciting new treasures to enjoy.

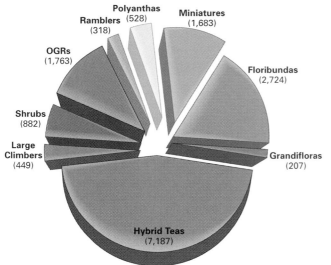

The number of roses throughout the world that are officially registered and commercially available in each classification gives clues to their popularity. At the present time the most popular roses are hybrid teas, floribundas, old garden roses, miniatures, and shrubs.

ROSE FAMILY TREE

The roses of yesteryear, collectively called old garden roses, were once grown by the European aristocracy. Although they went out of fashion for more than a century, old garden roses survived through the years in cottage gardens. Old garden roses have a long history. Three roses—the gallica rose (*Rosa gallica*), alba rose (*R. Alba*), and damask rose (*R. damascena*) are among the most ancient plants still cultivated. Grown in the Far and Near East during biblical times, these roses probably were carried to Western Europe by crusaders. The blood of the gallica rose, and perhaps the damask and alba roses, flows somewhere in the family tree of every known old garden or modern rose. During the Renaissance, roses became prized plants in the royalty's grand ornamental gardens and were no longer confined to apothecary cloistered gardens. The gardeners of the British, French, and Dutch aristocracy collected and hybridized roses during the 18th and 19th centuries, developing several dozen groups, many of which still can be found today. Cultivars in each group of old garden roses descend from the same species and bear a family resemblance to the group. The era of the modern rose began when the first hybrid tea rose was introduced in 1867. Bred from a tea rose and a hybrid perpetual rose, the hybrid tea rose seemed to be the ultimate in roses, featuring large, elegant, high-centered, fragrant blossoms that bloomed repeatedly from early summer through fall on reasonably cold-hardy plants. All the groups of roses developed after 1867 are termed modern roses. Groups developed prior to 1867, as well as new hybrids within these older groups, are termed old garden roses. Modern roses include hybrid teas, grandifloras, floribundas, miniatures, polyanthas, climbers, and the latest group—modern shrub roses, which combine old-garden-rose form and fragrance with modern colors and repeat blooms.

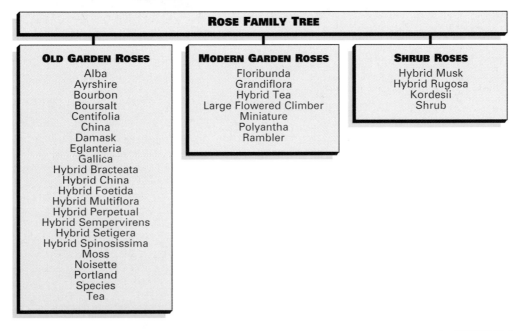

ROSE FAMILY TREE

OLD GARDEN ROSES	**MODERN GARDEN ROSES**	**SHRUB ROSES**
Alba	Floribunda	Hybrid Musk
Ayrshire	Grandiflora	Hybrid Rugosa
Bourbon	Hybrid Tea	Kordesii
Boursalt	Large Flowered Climber	Shrub
Centifolia	Miniature	
China	Polyantha	
Damask	Rambler	
Eglanteria		
Gallica		
Hybrid Bracteata		
Hybrid China		
Hybrid Foetida		
Hybrid Multiflora		
Hybrid Perpetual		
Hybrid Sempervirens		
Hybrid Setigera		
Hybrid Spinosissima		
Moss		
Noisette		
Portland		
Species		
Tea		

Rose Hardiness Zones

Pacific Northwest (PNW)

North Central (NC)

Pacific Southwest (PSW)

South Central (SC)

Roses and Your Climate

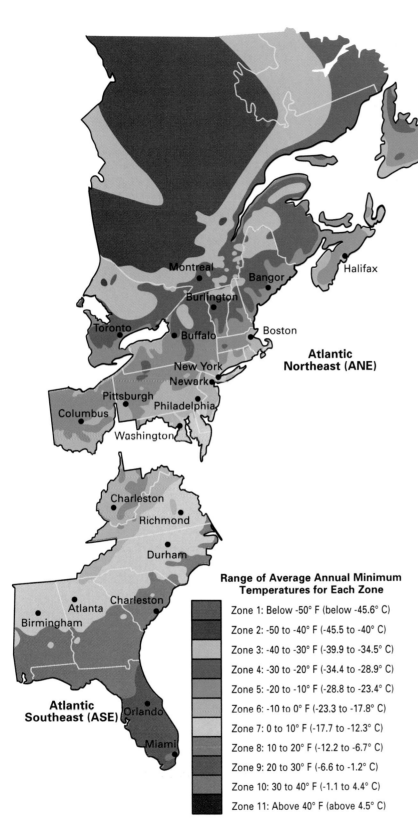

Atlantic Northeast (ANE)

Atlantic Southeast (ASE)

Range of Average Annual Minimum Temperatures for Each Zone

Zone 1: Below -50° F (below -45.6° C)

Zone 2: -50 to -40° F (-45.5 to -40° C)

Zone 3: -40 to -30° F (-39.9 to -34.5° C)

Zone 4: -30 to -20° F (-34.4 to -28.9° C)

Zone 5: -20 to -10° F (-28.8 to -23.4° C)

Zone 6: -10 to 0° F (-23.3 to -17.8° C)

Zone 7: 0 to 10° F (-17.7 to -12.3° C)

Zone 8: 10 to 20° F (-12.2 to -6.7° C)

Zone 9: 20 to 30° F (-6.6 to -1.2° C)

Zone 10: 30 to 40° F (-1.1 to 4.4° C)

Zone 11: Above 40° F (above 4.5° C)

Most roses are too tender for their above-ground growth to survive deep freezes. It is important to select roses that are proven performers in your climate. Some varieties require protection during cold winters, but they will survive mild winters quite easily. In areas where temperatures drop below 20° F, provide some measure of protection for most roses (see instructions for winter protection on pages 42 and 43). Still, many modern roses survive mild winter climates without any protection. If your climate is colder than this, consider the hardy old garden roses as well as shrub roses— or provide increased winter protection. The hardiest roses on the planet are the centifolias, albas, gallicas, and rugosas, all of which tolerate temperatures as low as -30° F with much above-ground growth intact.

HOW TO LOCATE YOUR HARDINESS ZONE

The USDA Agricultural Research Service climate map describes the normal average annual minimum temperature zones for the United States and Canada. The map at left divides much of North America into six regions for easier location of your zone: Atlantic Northeast (ANE), Atlantic Southeast (ASE), North Central (NC), South Central (SC), Pacific Northwest (PNW), and Pacific Southwest (PSW). For instance, in Chicago, Illinois (North Central region, or NC) the hardiness zone is 5—meaning the temperatures hit an average low during the winter months of -10° F to -20° F. In general, rose growers who live in or near zones 6 or colder need to provide some measure of winter protection and select roses that are not tender. In Zone 8 and south, no winter protection is generally needed except perhaps against sun, high temperatures, and strong winds.

REGIONAL WEATHER ZONES

In addition to hardiness zones, consider your region when selecting roses. Some varieties flourish in certain parts of the country and under-perform in others because of specific climatic conditions in a particular area. For example, a variety may perform well in Seattle and not so well in Dallas, even though they're in the same USDA zone. Entries in this guide list which of the six regional areas above are recommended, if it applies.

Hybrid Teas and Grandifloras

These are the long-stemmed roses you give (and receive) on Valentine's Day. Their cherished, perfectly pointed buds open to nodding but elegant blooms of pink, cream, apricot, and yellow. This is the most popular class of modern roses, with each bloom containing 25 to 50 petals on long stems, either singly or with several side buds. It is available in both bush and standard tree forms. The introduction of 'Peace' in 1945 heralded the modern era of the hybrid tea. It was overwhelmingly accepted and praised, and hybrid teas attained a zenith of symmetrical beauty. Recent All-America Rose Selections (AARS) in the hybrid tea class have been 'Double Delight', 'Olympiad', 'Sheer Bliss', 'Honor', 'Brigadoon', 'Secret'. In 1954, Walter Lammerts crossed the hybrid tea 'Charlotte Armstrong' with the floribunda 'Floradora', resulting in a carmine-rose and dawn-pink variety with the characteristics of a hybrid tea and the ability to bear clusters of flowers and grow to a commanding height of six to eight feet or more—and the resulting class called grandiflora was born. 'Queen Elizabeth' was the very first member of this class. Other popular varieties include 'Pink Parfait', 'Gold Medal', and 'Tournament of Roses'.

'Brandy' (1982); AARS. Rich mahogany-tinted foliage. Plant is tender and requires protection in winter climates. Spicy fragrance. 25 to 30 petals. Zones 6 to 11. RIR=7.0

'Brigadoon' (1992); AARS. Changes color as it opens from bud to bloom. Vigorous. Dark green foliage can be quite large in cooler climates. 35 to 40 petals. Zones 4 to 9. RIR=7.3

'Chrysler Imperial' (1953); AARS. Rich velvety blooms. Powerful fragrance. Likes heat in ASE, SC, and PSW. 45 to 50 petals. Zones 5 to 10. RIR=7.8

'Captain Harry Stebbings' (1980). Very large flowers especially in PNW, NC, and ANE. Blooms have classic hybrid-tea form. Tall, with a slightly spreading habit. Fruity, strong fragrance. 40 to 45 petals. Zones 5 to 10. RIR=8.0

'Crystalline' (1987). Originally bred for cut flowers. Heavy-toothed, medium-green foliage on a bush with grandiflora behavior. Spicy fragrance. 30 to 35 petals. Zones 5 to 10. RIR=8.4

'Double Delight' (1977); AARS. Elected to Rose Hall of Fame. Most popular rose of last 25 years. Vigorous. Beautiful foliage. Needs sun to develop full red color. Prone to mildew without protection. Spicy fragrance. Very tender; needs winter protection. 30 to 35 petals. Zones 6 to 10. RIR=8.7

'Dublin' (1982). Straight, strong stems bear large blooms. Needs humid warm evenings. 35 to 40 petals. Zones 5 to 10. RIR=8.6

'Elina' (1985). Boasts a luminescent charm. Tall and vigorous with loads of blossoms all summer and into fall. Very light fragrance. 30 to 35 petals. Zones 4 to 11. RIR=8.9

'Elegant Beauty' (1982). Blooms on long, elegant stems. Good for humid climates in SC and ASE. 30 to 35 petals. Zones 5 to 10. RIR=8.4

'Elizabeth Taylor' (1986). Shocking color with smoky edges. Prefers moderate to warm climates for best size. Light fragrance. 30 to 35 petals. Zones 5 to 10. RIR=8.9

'First Prize' (1970); AARS. Blooms are close to perfection, best in spring on established plants. Long, very thorny stems. Mild tea fragrance. 25 to 30 petals. Zones 5 to 10. RIR=8.6

Hybrid Teas and Grandifloras
continued

'Folklore' (1977). Perfect form. Stems tend to zig-zag rather than grow straight. Rich fragrance. 40 to 45 petals. Zones 4 to 11. RIR=8.5

'Fragrant Cloud' (1968). Elected to Rose Hall of Fame. Strong, spicy-sweet fragrance. Tall, vigorous, with dark glossy foliage. Responds well to harsh pruning after winter. 25 to 30 petals. Zones 4 to 11. RIR=8.1

'Gold Medal' (1986). Weather-proof blossoms. Tall, very vigorous. Colors are deeper in moderate climates. Best in PSW, SC, and ASE. 30 to 35 petals. Zones 5 to 10. RIR=8.6

'Granada' (1964); AARS. Blooms on long, straight stems. Keeps its color until blossom is spent. Heady perfume fragrance. PNW and PSW bring out the best. 25 to 30 petals. Zones 5 to 10. RIR=7.7

'Honor' (1980); AARS. Stately looking. Foliage is large and dark green, with good disease resistance. Stems tend to be too long at times. Prefers Pacific Coast regions. 25 to 30 petals. Zones 5 to 10. RIR=7.6

'Ingrid Bergman' (1985). Long, straight stems. Deep green, disease-resistant foliage. Tends to grow taller than other hybrid teas. Hardy, but a little heat improves color. 35 to 40 petals. Zones 4 to 11. RIR=7.1

'John F. Kennedy' (1965). Blooms are tough enough to survive cold or heat, but production can be disappointing. Moderate licorice fragrance. 40 to 50 petals. Zones 5 to 10. RIR=6.0

'Joyfulness' (1984). Classical shape. Large long-lasting blooms. Medium-size bush with strong straight stems against dark green foliage. 30 to 35 petals. Zones 5 to 10. RIR=8.3

'Just Joey' (1972); Elected to Rose Hall of Fame. Large ruffled flowers last for weeks with good color. Fruity fragrance. Vigorous and moderately hardy. 25 to 30 petals. Zones 5 to 10. RIR=7.9

'Kardinal' (1985). Originally bred for the cut flower industry. Small, perfect flower form. Outstanding in PNW. Vigorous grower. 30 to 35 petals. Zones 4 to 11. RIR=8.9

'Keepsake' (1981). Originally named 'Esmeralda'. Vigorous, disease resistant. Tends to spread a little rather than growing tall. Late bloomer in spring. Moderately hardy. 35 petals. Zones 5 to 10. RIR=8.9

'Louise Estes' (1994). Blooms ruffled at edges in some climates. Vigorous grower, tall, upright bush. Resistant to mildew. 40 to 45 petals. Zones 5 to 10. RIR=9.3

'Lynn Anderson' (1995). Large, attractive, closely stacked leaves. Long stems. Grooming helps bloom production. 25 to 30 petals. Zones 4 to 11

Hybrid Teas and Grandifloras
continued

'Marijke Koopman' (1979). An abundance of stems with perfectly formed blossoms all season. Light fragrance. Easy to grow, super clean. 25 petals. Zones 5 to 10. RIR=9.0

'Midas Touch' (1994); AARS. Color is non-fading, but not weatherproof. Blooms can open too fast in warmer climates. Prolific. 20 to 25 petals. Zones 4 to 11. RIR=7.6

'Mikado' (1988); AARS. Highly polished, medium-green foliage. Two-toned colors intensify spring and fall. Light, spicy fragrance. 30 to 35 petals. Zones 5 to 10. RIR=7.0

'Mister Lincoln' (1965); AARS. Tall, vigorous. Subject to infection by mildew if unprotected. Heavy damask fragrance. Best where days are warm and nights cool; PSW and SC. 30 to 35 petals. Zones 5 to 10. RIR=8.8

'New Zealand' (1995). Blooms have a great substance and form. Dark glossy foliage resists mildew. Bloom size best in cooler climates. Strong honeysuckle fragrance. 30 to 35 petals. Zones 5 to 10. RIR=7.1

'Opening Night' (1998); AARS. Simply sparkles. Strong, straight stems; foliage dark green and disease free. Prefers cooler temperatures. 25 to 30 petals. Zones 5 to 10

'Olympiad' (1984); AARS. A host of blossoms on a healthy, easy-to-grow bush. Large foliage is deeply veined, very disease resistant. 35 petals. Zones 5 to 10. RIR=9.0

'Paradise' (1978); AARS. Blooms are large but lack substance in dry hot climates like PSW. While heat enhances the blush, it can also burn foliage. 25 to 30 petals. Zones 5 to 8. RIR=7.1

'Perfect Moment' (1991); AARS. Large weather-proof, long-lasting blooms. Compact bush with dark green leaves. Disease resistant. Moderate summer temperatures give brightest colors. 25 to 30 petals. Zones 5 to 10. RIR=7.5

'Pink Parfait' (1961); AARS. Large clusters on medium-size, disease-resistant plant. Variety has been in commerce for more than 35 years. 25 to 30 petals. Zones 5 to 10. RIR=8.1

'Peace' (1946); AARS. Established the hybrid-tea standards in the 20th century. Opulent blossoms. Foliage is large, glossy green. Easy to grow. Very fragrant. Color is best east of the Rockies in NC and SC. 40 to 45 petals. Zones 5 to 9. RIR=8.4

'Pristine' (1978). Large, substantial blossoms on strong, very thorny stems open quickly but last only a few days. Foliage is thick and disease free. 25 to 30 petals. Zones 5 to 10. RIR=9.1

'Queen Elizabeth' (1955); AARS. Elected to Rose Hall of Fame. The first grandiflora. Large trusses of blooms on strong, straight stems. Color is clear, weatherproof in any climate. A climbing counterpart exists. 35 petals. Zones 5 to 10. RIR=7.4

'Rina Hugo' (1993). Officially a hybrid tea rose, but produces large clusters of heavy blooms in any climate. 40 to 50 petals. Zones 5 to 10.

Hybrid Teas and Grandifloras
continued

'Royal Highness' *(1963); AARS. Graceful blooms seem porcelain on dark glossy foliage. Color and size improves in moderate climates. 40 to 45 petals. Zones 5 to 10. RIR=7.8*

'Secret' *(1994); AARS. Well-formed blossoms on strong stems. Mahogany-red new foliage. Easy to grow. Sweet and spicy fragrance. 30 to 35 petals. Color is best in cool climates like PSW and ANE. Zones 5 to 10. RIR=7.7*

'Sheer Bliss' *(1987); AARS. Tall bush, stiff glossy green foliage mildews if unprotected. Blooms can suffer in mild rainfall. Best in dry sunny climates, such as PSW and ASE. 35 petals. Zones 5 to 10. RIR=7.8*

'Sheer Elegance' *(1991); AARS. Abundance of blooms on straight stems all year long. Best grown in cooler climates for maximum size and color. 30 to 35 petals. Zones 5 to 10. RIR=7.7*

'Signature' *(1996). Blooms singly on strong, straight stems. Dark green foliage. Compact bush. Lower foliage tends to drop after the first bloom. Light and fruity fragrance. 30 to 35 petals. Zones 5 to 10.*

'St. Patrick' *(1996); AARS. Moderately hardy. Novel flower form surrounded by chartreuse foliage. Heat brings out color. Vigorous. Performs best in southern states in fall. 30 to 35 petals. Zones 5 to 10.*

'Stainless Steel' *(1997). Elegantly-formed blossom with mysterious colors. Tall, upright bush; foliage can mildew unless protected. Color is best in cool climates. 25 to 30 petals. Zones 5 to 10.*

'Sunset Celebration' (1998); AARS. The Golden Rose of The Hague Award (Holland). Covered with fragrant blooms ranging from cool to warm tones. Colors are deeper in cool conditions such as the ANE. Easy to grow. 35 to 40 petals. Zones 5 to 10.

'Touch of Class' (1986); AARS. Keeps its form for weeks. Weather-proof blooms. Foliage mildews if unprotected. Color fades in hot sunny climates of PSW and SC. 30 petals. Zones 6 to 11. RIR=9.3

'Timeless' (1997); AARS. Blooms take a long time to open fully, but worth the wait. Medium-sized and compact. Disease resistant. Prefers milder temperature in NC and ANE. 25 petals. Zones 4 to 11

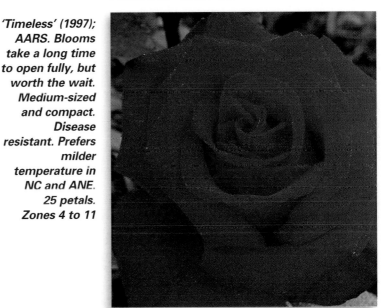

'Tournament of Roses' (1989); AARS. Florets borne in large sprays cover the bush. Color can improve with some warmth. 25 to 30 petals. Zones 5 to 10. RIR=8.0

'Tropicana' (1963); AARS. The luminous blooms of this historic hybrid tea demand attention. Sweet, fruity fragrance. Performs best east of the Rockies. 30 to 35 petals. Zones 5 to 10. RIR=7.5

'Uncle Joe' (1972). Large blooms, good color, perfect flower form in warm, humid climates. Strong straight stems. Blooms do not open fully in dry warm climates like PSW. 50+ petals. Zones 5 to 10. RIR=8.1

'Valencia' (1989). Blooms can be as big as dinner plates. Long-lasting on bush or in the home. Large leaves are disease free. Strong fragrance. 35 to 40 petals. Zones 5 to 10.

Floribundas and Polyanthas

Second only to the hybrid tea in popularity, the floribundas flower in large clusters, with smaller individual blossoms (2 to 3 inches in diameter) than those of the hybrid teas. Floribundas are usually 3 to 4 feet tall and work best when used at the front of a bed or border—or as a hedge. This class is unrivaled for providing massive, frequent, long-lasting, colorful garden displays. Floribundas as a class are somewhat hardier, easier to care for, and more reliable in wet weather than their hybrid tea cousins. Recent AARS winners include 'Class Act', 'Impatient', 'Intrigue', 'Sun Flare', 'French Lace', 'Cherish', 'First Edition', 'Brass Band', and 'Singin' in the Rain'. 'Playboy' is a slightly fragrant scarlet-and-gold variety hybridized by Cocker of Aberdeen, Scotland, in 1975. Two new seedlings from 'Playboy' have appeared, 'Playgirl' and 'Playfair', both single-petaled varieties on the same theme but with dramatic color blends. Polyanthas are bushy, 2-foot plants that were developed in the late 19th century with crosses of the multiflora with hybrid teas. With their narrow, finely textured leaves and clusters of 1-inch blossoms, they are sturdy, trouble-free plants for massing, edgings, and hedges.

'Amber Queen' (1988); AARS. Glossy disease-resistant foliage. Color is lighter in cooler climates and darker with warm and humid nights. Low- to medium-size bush, 2 to 3 feet tall. 25 to 30 petals. Zones 5 to 10. RIR=6.5

'Angel Face' (1969); AARS. Blooms have a ruffled edge. Plants take two seasons to establish before producing massive displays of sprays. Bush is low and rounded, 4 feet tall. Strong citrus fragrance. A climbing counterpart is available. 25 to 30 petals. Zones 5 to 10. RIR=7.8

'Anthony Meilland' (1995). This unfading floribunda continuously produces elegant clusters of large double flowers. Blooms have a light fragrance. Bush is vigorous, symmetrical, and mounded, 4 to 5 feet tall, with ample foliage. 25 to 30 petals. Zones 5 to 10.

'Apricot Nectar' (1966); AARS. Large blossoms. Glossy dark green, disease-resistant foliage, 3 to 4 feet tall. Fragrant. 30 to 40 petals. Zones 5 to 10. RIR=8.0

''Betty Boop' (1999); AARS. Plant is self-cleaning with a fast recycle time. Performs well in nearly all climates. A superb informal hedge, 4 to 5 feet tall. 6 to 12 petals. Zones 5 to 10.

'Betty Prior' (1938). Nonstop clusters spring to fall, great for massing. 5 to 6 feet tall. Vigorous, winter hardy. A climbing counterpart is available. 5 to 7 petals. Zones 4 to 10. RIR=8.2

'Blueberry Hill' (1997). Upright on strong, straight stems, 4 to 5 feet tall. Good resistance to mildew. Fragrance resembles apple tart. 12 to 15 petals. Zones 5 to 10.

'Brass Band' (1995); AARS. Well-formed blooms in small clusters. Cool weather improves size and color. Fruity fragrance. 30 to 35 petals. Zones 5 to 10. RIR=7.8

'Cherish' (1980); AARS. Small clusters of perfect flowers. Vigorous. Disease resistant. Good for cut flowers. 25 to 30 petals. Zones 4 to 11. RIR=7.7

'Circus' (1956); AARS. Blooms in giant sprays on a 4- to 5-foot bush. Colors are brighter in cooler temperatures. A climbing form is available. Spicy fragrance. 40 to 45 petals. Zones 5 to 10. RIR=6.8

'Class Act' (1989); AARS. Blooms in small clusters. Weatherproof. Upright compact bush 4 to 5 feet tall. Fruity fragrance. 15 to 20 petals. Zones 5 to 10. RIR=7.6

'Columbus' (1992). Hybrid-tea-size flowers in small sprays. Medium-rounded bush. Consistent performer in most climates. Slight fragrance. 30 to 35 petals. Zones 5 to 10. RIR=7.3

'Dicky' (1984); Royal National Rose Society Gold Medal (England). Bred in Northern Ireland. Large clusters. Light fragrance. 35+ petals. Zones 5 to 10. RIR=8.8

Floribundas and Polyanthas
continued

'Else Poulsen' *(1924). Simple form. Bush covers itself with flower sprays all year. Vigorous, 4 to 6 feet tall. 10 petals. Zones 5 to 10. RIR=8.1*

'Europeana' *(1968); AARS. Produces massive sprays of red blossoms all season long. Glossy, disease-resistant foliage. Prefers heat. 25 to 30 petals. Zones 5 to 10. RIR=9.0*

'Fashion' *(1950); AARS. Sweet fragrance. Vigorous, medium-size bush. Large blooms in cool climates (PNW). 20 to 25 petals. Zones 5 to 10. RIR=7.8*

'First Edition' *(1977); AARS. Small clusters of delicate blossoms. Glossy, dark green foliage. Compact medium-size bush, 4 to 5 feet tall. Light tea fragrance. 28 to 30 petals. Zones 5 to 10. RIR=8.4*

'First Kiss' *(1991). Compact clusters of delicate blossoms on strong stems. Medium-green foliage on compact bush, 3 to 4 feet tall. Best in cooler climates, PNW and ANE. 5 to 25 petals. Zones 5 to 10. RIR=8.1*

'French Lace' *(1982); AARS. Small clusters of delicate, well-formed hybrid-tea-size blooms. Best color and performance in cooler climates (PSW, NC, and ASE.). Protect over winter. 30 to 35 petals. Zones 5 to 10. RIR=8.3*

'Gene Boerner' *(1969); AARS. Tall upright bushes with perfect blooms in large clusters. Deepest colors in spring and fall. Spicy fragrance. 35 to 40 petals. Zones 5 to 10. RIR=8.5*

'Iceberg' *(1958); Rose Hall of Fame. Very profuse bloomer. Masses of large trusses constantly cover the bush. Hardy. Also available in a climbing counterpart. 20 to 25 petals. Zones 4 to 10. RIR=8.9*

'Impatient' *(1984); AARS. Low-maintenance; provides fiery clusters all season. Tall to medium upright plant 4 feet high. Warmer climates (ASE and SC) improve brightness of the color. 25 petals. Zones 5 to 10. RIR=7.7*

'Ivory Fashion' (1959); AARS. Large, well-formed blooms in medium-size clusters all year. Dark leathery foliage. Vigorous. Nearly thornless stems. Best in cooler climates such as NC and ANE. 17 petals. Zones 5 to 10. RIR=8.3

'Katherine Locker' (1978). Perfectly formed solitary or clustered blooms. Dark green, healthy foliage. Non-fading color, even in strong sunlight. Cool temperatures improve color and size. 28 petals. Zones 5 to 10. RIR=7.3

'Lavaglut' (1978). Large flowers in great clusters on strong stems. Contrasting yellow stamens. Hardy but prefers PNW and NC. 24 petals. Zones 4 to 11. RIR=8.9

'Little Darling' (1956). Perfectly formed blossoms are produced in clusters of 10 to 20. Plant can get 3 to 4 feet tall and wide in warm climates. Hardy: Survives Great Lakes winters. 25 to 30 petals. Zones 4 to 10. RIR=8.3

'Livin' Easy' (1996); AARS. Neon colors. Vigorous, disease resistant. Easy to grow. Does well in a wide range of climates. Fragrant. 25 to 30 petals. Zones 5 to 10.

'Margaret Merrill' (1978). Perfectly shaped weather-proof blooms. Vigorous, disease resistant. Tough deep-green foliage. Rich citrus and spice fragrance. 15 to 20 petals. Zones 5 to 10. RIR=8.5

'Marina' (1981); AARS. Originally introduced as a cut flower. Massive sprays of blossoms. Flower size increases with cooler days. 35 to 40 petals. Zones 5 to 10. RIR=7.3

'Matador' (1972). Flashing blooms in medium-size clusters. Leathery, dark green foliage on upright bush. Prefers cool climates like the NC. 25 to 30 petals. Zones 5 to 10. RIR=6.1

'Nicole' (1985). Tall with elegant clusters. Strong, thorny stems. Tough, leathery dark foliage. Disease resistant. Grows well all climates. 20 to 25 petals. Zones 5 to 10. RIR=9.2

Floribundas and Polyanthas
continued

'Permanent Wave' (1935). Nearly always covered with large sprays. Vigorous, prolific. A magnet to mildew if left unprotected. Hardy. Does best in NC and ANE. 10 petals. Zones 4 to 10. RIR=7.3

'Playboy' (1976). Bountiful sprays of 5 to 9 blooms. Glossy, dark green foliage on tall, 6-foot, upright plant. Does well in all climates. Apple fragrance. 7 to 10 petals. Zones 4 to 11. RIR=8.1

'Playgirl' (1986). Offspring of 'Playboy'. Contrasting golden stamens. Glossy foliage. Vigorous in most climates. 5 to 7 petals. Zones 5 to 10. RIR=8.1

'Pleasure' (1990); AARS. Small clusters of blossoms. Slow to establish. Best color in cooler climates. Light fragrance. 30 to 35 petals. Zones 5 to 10. RIR=7.9

'Purple Tiger' (1991). Large blooms in small clusters. Near- thornless stems. Vigorous, 3 to 4 feet tall. 20 to 25 petals. Zones 5 to 10. RIR=7.4

'Regensberg' (1979). Compact, loaded with blossoms through summer. Blooms larger in cooler climates. Sweet apple fragrance. 30 to 35 petals. Zones 5 to 10. RIR=8.2

'Scentimental' 1997; AARS. Medium-size sprays of 5 to 11 blooms (no two alike). Spicy fragrance. Prefers NC and PNW. 25 to 30 petals. Zones 4 to 11.

'Sexy Rexy' (1984). High candelabras of 40 to 50 blooms on strong, straight stems. Hardy, survives most climates. 30 to 40 petals. Zones 4 to 10. RIR=9.0

'Sheila's Perfume' (1985). Wonderful flower and fruit. Blooms more hybrid-tea-sized. Vigorous, compact. Glossy, dark green foliage. Fragrant. 25 petals. Zones 5 to 10. RIR=8.3

'Shocking Blue' (1974). Blooms in small attractive clusters. Larger blooms in cooler climates, ANE and NC. Strong citrus fragrance. 25 to 30 petals. Zones 5 to 10. RIR=7.0

'Showbiz' (1985); AARS. Outstanding bright color on large trusses of blooms. Takes a season to establish. Disease resistant. 20 to 25 petals. Zones 5 to 10. RIR=8.6

'Singin' in the Rain' (1995); AARS. Interesting color combinations vary with climate—from brown and cinnamon-pink to apricot-gold and russet-orange. Blooms are weatherproof. Musk fragrance. 25 to 30 petals. Zones 5 to 10. RIR=8.2

'Summer Fashion' (1986). Bloom radiates color. Fruity fragrance. A little heat intensifies the color. 35 to 40 petals. Zones 5 to 10. RIR=7.6

'Sunsprite' (1977). Consistently voted one of 10 best yellow roses in the world. Deep non-fading color. Glossy green foliage. Disease resistant. Prefers cooler climates, PNW and NC. Super-sweet fragrance. 25 to 30 petals. Zones 5 to 10. RIR=8.7

'Sun Flare' (1983); AARS. Often appears in top 10 lists. Mounded bushes covered with flowers. Foliage is polished green and disease resistant. Light licorice fragrance. 25 to 30 petals. Zones 5 to 10. RIR=8.3

'Sweet Vivian' (1961). Small clusters of delicately colored blooms on long stems suitable for cutting. Dark green, disease-resistant foliage. Best in moderate climates. 12 to 15 petals. Zones 5 to 10. RIR=8.0

'The Fairy' (1932). A classic, trouble-free polyantha for nearly endless flowers. Small ruffled flowers in large trusses bow elegantly from their weight. Grows 4 to 5 feet tall and wide if allowed to spread. Hardy and clean. 20 to 25 petals. Zones 5 to 10. RIR=8.7

'Trumpeter' (1977). Long-lasting blooms. Attractive glossy foliage. Great for mass planting. Likes just a little heat. 35 to 40 petals. Zones 5 to 10. RIR=8.0

Miniatures

Miniature roses provide novelty, versatility, color range, availability, and ease of cultivation. They can be massed in beds or as ground cover, used for edging beds, growing in containers and rockeries, and even taken indoors as temporary pot plants. The maximum height of the average miniature rose plant is about 15 inches. They are usually sold in 4-inch pots ready for transplanting. Miniature roses are grown on their own roots and are hardier than either hybrid teas or floribundas. Generally, miniature roses are available year-round from mail-order sources.

Flower form and foliage are miniature versions of both hybrid teas and floribundas. Miniatures introduced recently that exhibit the classic hybrid tea form are 'Minnie Pearl', 'Jean Kenneally', 'Loving Touch', 'Rainbow's End', 'Snow Bride', and 'Irresistible'. Old favorites include 'Party Girl', 'Rise 'n' Shine', 'Starina', 'Magic Carrousel', and 'Peaches 'n' Cream'.

Single-petaled miniature roses such as 'Why Not' have been extremely popular. There is new respect for varieties that do not possess the classic hybrid tea form. Varieties that have gained the most popularity are 'Green Ice' and 'Gourmet Popcorn'. The latest introduction is the very fragrant 'Sweet Chariot' by Ralph Moore. Heavy with fragrance, this variety is ideal for a hanging basket.

'American Rose Centennial' (1991). Beautifully formed blossoms, one to a stem or in small clusters. Vigorous, compact bush. Dark green foliage. 20 to 30 petals. Zones 5 to 10. RIR=6.3

'Behold' (1997). Giant clusters of perfectly formed blossoms on long, strong stems. Vigorous. 15 to 20 petals. Zones 4 to 11.

'Black Jade' (1985); AOE. Tall vigorous upright bush throws out clusters on strong, straight stems. Contrasting yellow stamens. 30 petals. Zones 5 to 10. RIR=8.3

'Carrot Top' (1994). Clusters of stunning color on stems often not strong enough to support the weight of the blossoms. Vigorous grower. Repeat blooms fairly well. 20 to 25 petals. Zones 5 to 10. RIR=7.8

'Glowing Amber' (1997). Perfectly formed blooms, vivid color combinations on long, delicate stems. Prolific. 25 to 30 petals. Zones 4 to 11.

'Gourmet Popcorn' (1986). Masses of sprays (30 to 60 blooms) cover a vigorous bush. Shiny dark green foliage. Disease resistant. Hardy. 12 to 20 petals. Zones 4 to 10. RIR=8.7

'Green Ice' (1971). Green-tinged before blooms open. Large trusses make this ideal for hanging baskets. Can sprawl and spread. 30 to 35 petals. Zones 4 to 10. RIR=7.6

'Hot Tamale' (1994). Single blooms in warm climates, small sprays where cooler. Vigorous spreader to 3 feet tall. 25 petals. Zones 5 to 10. RIR=8.1

'Incognito' (1997). Blossom color varies somewhat from dusty-mauve to hints of yellow, pink, and russet. Vigorous medium-size bush. Seems to always be in bloom. 25 petals. Zones 5 to 10.

'Irresistible' (1976); AOE. Vigorous; 3 feet tall. Perfect, long-lasting blooms grow in candelabras. 45 to 50 petals. Zones 5 to 10. RIR=9.4

'Jean Kenneally' (1986); AOE. Tall, elegant sprays of exquisitely shaped apricot blossoms. Thrives in just about all climates. Blooms are close to perfection. 25 petals. Zones 5 to 10. RIR=9.5

'Jeanne LaJoie' (1977); AOE. Climber. Abundant non-fading blooms if canes are trained horizontally. Vigorous, hardy. 40 petals. Zones 4 to 11. RIR=9.3

'June Laver' (1987). Terrific form of blossoms and excellent color on low-growing, short stems. Production can be lean. Not especially hardy. 20 to 25 petals. Zones 6 to 11. RIR=7.7

'Kristin' (1993); AOE. Great color combination on a vigorous plant; intensifies in hot climates. Disease resistant. In cooler climates blooms tend not to open fully. 27 to 30 petals. Zones 5 to 10. RIR=7.9

Miniatures
continued

'Little Artist' (1982). Low, spreading canopy of unique blossoms, each with a different pattern, is ideal for containers. Hardy. 14 to 21 petals. Zones 4 to 10. RIR=8.8

'Loving Touch' (1985); AOE. Wonderful color with dark green foliage. Bloom size is large in cool climates. Tall, upright bush. 25 petals. Zones 5 to 10. RIR=8.5

'Luis Desamero' (1989). Perfect blooms grow one to a stem. Tall, upright, healthy, and vigorous. Abundant foliage sets. 28 petals. Zones 5 to 10. RIR=7.7

'Magic Carousel' (1975); AOE. Striking color combination. Beautiful display when fully open. Vigorous and hardy. 25 petals. Zones 5 to 10. RIR=8.9

'Mary Marshall' (1975); AOE. Easy to maintain. Abundant, fast-repeating blooms. Dwarf-like, disease free. Climbing counterpart also available. 20 to 25 petals. Zones 5 to 10. RIR=7.6

'Minnie Pearl' (1982). Blooms singly or in large clusters. Glossy foliage; flower form holds even in heat conditions. Vigorous. Hardy. 25 to 30 petals. Zones 4 to 10. RIR=9.5

'Miss Flippins' (1997). Blooms hold classic form for days. Foliage is large but balanced with bloom size. Vigorous grower, 2 to 3 feet tall and wide. 20 petals. Zones 5 to 10.

'Old Glory' (1988); AOE. Hybrid tea form; single in warm climates, clustered in cool areas. Flowers age gracefully. Vigorous. 23 to 25 petals. Zones 4 to 11. RIR=7.8

'Party Girl' (1982); AOE. Immaculate flower form on large candelabras with as many as 20 florets at a time. Performs best in cooler climates. Not hardy. 23 petals. Zones 6 to 10. RIR=8.7

'Peaches 'n' Cream' (1977); AOE. Tapered buds open to full blossom. In cold, damp climates florets will not open fully. Vigorous and compact. 50+ petals. Zones 5 to 10. RIR=8.0

'Pinstripe' (1986). Myriad fully opened, long-lasting blooms, each with different markings. Low mounded habit. Dense, disease-resistant foliage. 35 petals. Zones 5 to 10. RIR=8.1

'Rainbow's End' (1986); AOE. Upright bush with blooms on short stems. Ideal for containers. Climbing counterpart recently available. 35 petals. Zones 5 to 10. RIR=9.0

'Rise 'n' Shine' (1978); AOE. Brilliant clear timeless yellow blossoms. Dark, glossy green foliage. Medium-size bush. 35 petals. Zones 5 to 10. RIR=8.8

'Roller Coaster' (1987). Striped blossoms, no two exactly alike, grow in small clusters. A novelty rose. Hardy. 6 to 14 petals. Zones 4 to 10. RIR=8.0

'Scentsational' (1997). Great flower form, substance, and vigor, but can be a bit large in cooler climates. Fragrant. Tall. 30 to 35 petals. Zones 5 to 10.

'Snow Bride' (1983); AOE. Petals reflex to give porcelain-like qualities to marvelous blooms. Survives heat and cold. Compact, low growing. Disease resistant. 20 petals. Zones 5 to 10. RIR=9.0

'Starina' (1965). Blooms singly or in small clusters of 3 to 5 florets. An international award-winning rose. Dwarf habit. 20 petals. Zones 5 to 10. RIR=8.7

'Sweet Chariot' (1984). Small florets have informal old garden form. Ideal for a hanging basket. Heavy damask fragrance. 40 petals. Zones 5 to 10. RIR=8.0

'Why Not' (1983). Upright bush. Fast rebloomer. Small blooms and matte-finish foliage. Color fades after a few days. Light fragrance. 5 petals. Zones 5 to 10. RIR=7.9

'X-Rated' (1993). Excellent flower form on large candelabras. Intense in cooler climates. Light fragrance. 26 to 40 petals. Zones 5 to 10.

Species and Old Garden Roses

Grow some history in your garden! Species roses—as their name implies—were the first wild roses, from which all the old garden roses and, eventually, the modern roses were bred. Old roses are often referred to as heritage roses or old-fashioned roses. In 1966 the American Rose Society defined old garden roses as those varieties that existed prior to 1867, the year of the first hybrid tea. Certain old garden roses have been introduced after 1867, but if they belong to an established classification existing prior to 1867, they are still classified as old garden roses. There are several distinguishing features that set old garden roses apart from all others. After an initial spring crop, they usually don't produce any more flowers. But their hip production adds a distinct beauty to the fall garden. Few are considered recurrent bloomers. Flower form can be quartered, cupped, imbricated or expanded, reflexed, globular, or compact. The beauty of old garden roses often lies in the heavy fragrance these roses can impart to the garden. Within this general category are the following subdivisions:

ALBA: Once-blooming, upright habit, dense foliage, very hardy, and disease resistant. Alba means white. Hardy to zone 3.

BOURBON: Repeat-blooming plants, 2 to 15 feet tall, fragrant, quartered blooms. Zone 5 with protection.

CENTIFOLIA: Four to 8 feet tall, once-blooming, very fragrant. Centifolia means 100 petals. Hardy to zone 4.

CHINA: One to 3 feet tall, with somewhat weak stems. Clusters of blossoms, repeat-blooming, spicy fragrance. Zone 6 with protection.

DAMASK: Intense, heavy fragrance, 3 to 6 feet tall. Some are repeat-blooming. Zone 5 with protection.

GALLICA: Small (3 to 4 feet tall) bushy plants. Once-blooming, fragrant, brilliant colors. Hardy to zone 4.

HYBRID PERPETUAL: Repeat-blooming, 6 feet tall. Fragrant, mostly in pinks and reds. Hardiness varies.

MOSS: Three to 6 feet tall, some repeat bloomers. Mossy growth on penduncle and sepals, fragrant. Hardy to zone 4.

NOISETTE: Rambles up to 20 feet. Large, repeat-blooming, clusters of blossoms. Very fragrant. Zone 7.

PORTLAND: Four feet tall, repeat-blooming plants, short penduncles. Fragrant. Zone 5 with protection.

TEA: About 4 feet tall, large blooms, weak stems, fragrant, repeat-blooming. Some climb. Zones 7 to 10.

'Apothecary's Rose' (pre-1600); gallica (Rosa gallica officinalis), also known as "Red Rose of Lancaster." Erect growth, 3 feet tall. Can spread by suckers. Blooms are prolific in spring. Semi-double, 35 to 40 petals. Zones 4 to 10. RIR=8.7

'Archduke Charles' (1840); china. Recurrent bloomer all summer. Color intensifies with age. Disease resistant. Vigorous bush, 2 to 3 feet tall. Intense fragrance. 30 to 40 petals. Zones 5 to 10. RIR=8.3

"Austrian Copper" (pre-1590); species. Officially known as Rosa foetida bicolor. Blooms once in the spring but the display is dazzling. Grows 4 feet tall (taller in warm climates). 5 petals. Zones 4 to 11. RIR=7.7

'Autumn Damask' (1819); damask (also know as "Quatre Saisons"). Large florets with sometimes crumpled petals on 4-foot-tall plant. Flowering is best in spring and late fall. Highly fragrant. 35 to 40 petals. Zones 5 to 11. RIR=8.2

'Baron Girod de l'Ain' (1897); hybrid perpetual. Repeat blooming. Petals have ragged white deckle edge. Healthy looking 4-foot bush. Fragrant. 30 to 40 petals. Zones 5 to 10. RIR=7.1

'Baronne Prevost' (1842); hybrid perpetual. Big, flat, open flowers are quartered with a button eye. Erect, bushy 4- to 6-foot-tall plant. Recurrent bloomer. Rich fragrance. 100+ petals. Zones 5 to 10. RIR=8.7

'Boule de Neige' (1867); bourbon. Repeat blooming. Name means "snowballs." Leathery foliage, 4 to 5 feet tall, disease resistant. Fragrant. 100+ petals. Zones 5 to 10 (with protection). RIR=7.7

'Cardinal de Richelieu' (1840); gallica. One bloom cycle on 4- to 5-foot plant during the spring and summer but worth the color display. Sweet fragrance. 40 to 50 petals. Zones 4 to 9. RIR=7.8

'Catherine Mermet' (1869); tea. Blooms spring through fall with shapely florets. Flower size can vary with climate. Coppery-tinged foliage is 4 feet tall and disease resistant. Light fragrance. 25 to 30 petals. Zones 7 to 10. RIR=7.5.

'Celestial' (pre-1848); alba. Open blooms, golden stamens. Gray-green foliage. Fragrant, vigorous, 6 feet. 25 to 30 petals. Zones 5 to 9. RIR=8.6

'Celine Forestier' (1858); noisette. Abundant large, flat, fragrant flowers with muddled centers nearly year round. Vigorous. Can be cultivated as a small climber. 6 to 7 feet tall. 50+ petals. Zones 7 to 10. RIR=9.9

'Charles de Mills' (date of origin unknown); gallica. Vigorous and fragrant. One bloom cycle in late spring, early summer. Requires good soil conditions. 4 to 5 feet tall. 40 to 50 petals. Zones 4 to 9. RIR=8.6

Old Garden Roses
continued

'Comte de Chambord' (1860). Attractive quartered-flower form, heavy old rose perfume. Disease resistant. Blooms constantly. Plant is vigorous and of medium height. 40 to 50 petals. Zones 5 to 9. RIR=8.0.

'Crested Moss' (1827); moss. Also known as "Chapeau de Napoleon." One bloom cycle in the spring and summer. Buds resemble cocked-hats. In warm climates can be grown as small climber, 5 to 6 feet tall. Very fragrant. 35 to 40 petals. Zones 5 to 9. RIR=8.7.

'Duchesse de Brabant' (1857); tea. Ample supply of shapely florets late spring into fall. Small, well-foliated bush with a spreading habit, 3 to 4 feet tall. Strong fragrance. 45 to 50 petals. Zones 5 to 11. RIR=8.6.

'Enfant de France' (1860); hybrid perpetual. Huge, satiny blossoms all year. Small, dense bush with lots of foliage, 3 feet tall. Very fragrant. 40 to 50 petals. Zones 4 to 9. RIR=8.6

'Felicite Parmentier' (1834); alba. Tidy bush to 4 feet tall with dark grayish-green foliage. Very strong fragrance. 40 to 50 petals. Zones 5 to 9. RIR=8.7

'Ferdinand Pichard' (1921); hybrid perpetual. One of the few striped old garden roses to repeat bloom. Tall, upright plant with disease-resistant foliage, 6 feet tall. Distinct fragrance. 25 petals. Zones 4 to 9. RIR=6.8

'Great Maiden's Blush' (pre-1738); alba. Also known as "Cuisse de Nymph Emue." Loose flower form, surrounded by blue-gray leaves. Blooms once. Grows 6 feet tall. Strong, sweet fragrance. 35 to 40 petals. Zones 5 to 9. RIR=9.1

'Irene Watts' (1896); china. Blooms all year with clusters of pompon-like florets. Foliage is dark green margined with purple. Vigorous, 3 feet tall. 35 to 40 petals. Zones 7 to 9

'Ispahan' (pre-1823); damask. Extended blooming in early summer. Blooms hold their color well in the sun. Attractive foliage. Stems not too thorny, 5 feet tall. Very fragrant. 35 to 40 petals. Zones 5 to 9. RIR=8.4

'Konigin von Danemark' (1826); alba. Small florets quartered with a button center. Blooms once in summer. Great fragrance. Blue-green foliage, 5 to 6 feet tall. 50 petals. Zones 4 to 10. RIR=8.6

'La Belle Sultane' (1795); gallica. Lovely, but one-time-only display of semi-double florets. Contrasting yellow stamens. Tall, 5 to 6 feet and upright. 7 to 15 petals. Zones 4 to 10. RIR=8.0

'Louise Odier' (1851); bourbon. Fragrant blossoms resembling camellias in clusters often too heavy for the stems to support. Blooms spring into fall. 6 feet tall. 5 to 40 petals. Zones 5 to 10. RIR=8.5

'Madame Hardy' (1832); damask. Rich green central pip with petals folded inward. Blooms once in spring. Strong scent. Grows 5 to 6 feet tall. 100 petals or more. Zones 5 to 11. RIR=9.0

'Madame Alfred Carriere' (1879); noisette. Climber with continuous recurrent flowering. Large florets, rather loosely formed. 10 to 12 feet tall. Strong fragrance. 35 to 40 petals. Zones 6 to 10. RIR=9.0

'Madame Pierre Oger' (1878); bourbon. Florets resemble translucent water lilies. Very fragrant. Recurrent bloomer. Vigorous, hardy, and disease resistant. 5 feet tall. 35 to 40 petals. Zones 6 to 10. RIR=8.0

'Madame Isaac Pereire' (1881); bourbon. This bold, tall bush blooms spring to fall on strong stems. Strong fragrance. Can be trained as a climber in warmer climates, 7 to 8 feet tall. 40 petals. Zones 6 to 10. RIR=8.4

Old Garden Roses
continued

'Marechal Niel' (1864); noisette. Climber. Florets in clusters, very fragrant. Foliage is dark coppery green. Vigorous, to 15 feet tall. Prefers heat. 35 to 40 petals. Zones 5 to 11. RIR=7.4

'Mermaid' (1918); hybrid bracteata. Large, fragrant, single-petaled blossoms appear spring to fall. Beautiful climber, 20 to 30 feet tall. Watch out for thorns! Tender in cold climates. 5 petals. Zones 5 to 11. RIR=8.5

'Mrs. B.R. Cant' (1901); tea. Free-flowering throughout the season. Vigorous, disease resistant, 3 to 4 feet tall. A climbing counterpart is also available. Fragrant. 35 to 40 petals. Zones 7 to 9. RIR=8.7

'Old Blush' (1752); china. Thornless, recurrent bloomer to 4 feet tall. A climbing form for zones 8 to 10 is available. 25 to 30 petals. Zones 7 to 9 with protection. RIR=8.1

'Paul Neyron' (1869); hybrid perpetual. Huge florets with cupped form come singly on strong, straight stems. Bloom is intermittent, lightly scented. Plants grow 6 feet tall. 50 petals. Zones 5 to 9. RIR=8.1

'Reine Victoria' (1872); bourbon. Slender, erect bush with perpetual supply of cupped florets, usually in small clusters. Light fragrance. 4 to 5 feet tall. 25 to 30 petals. Zones 5 to 9 (needs protection). RIR=8.0

'Reine des Violettes' (1860); hybrid perpetual. Unusual violet blooms appear spring to fall, shatter easily after a few days. Upright climbing plant with few thorns, 6 to 8 feet tall. Great fragrance. 75 petals. Zones 5 to 9. RIR=8.0

'Reve d'Or' (1869); noisette. Shapely blossoms can have a tinge of pink in cooler climates. Some recurrent blooming. Very fragrant. Vigorous but tender climber, 12 feet tall. 25 to 30 petals. Zones 7 to 9. RIR=9.4

'Rose de Meaux' (1789); centifolia. Fragrant flowers have frilly petals and pompon form. Only one bloom cycle in early summer. Dwarf bush with erect stems, 3 feet tall. 25 to 30 petals. Zones 4 to 9. RIR=7.2

'Rose de Rescht' (1940); damask. Small 3-foot bush. Florets are a tight rosette. Fragrant. 50+ petals. Zones 5 to 9. RIR=8.9

'Rose du Roi' (1815); portland. Dwarf compact bush, 3 feet tall. Recurrent blooming, very fragrant. Prefers mild climates. 25 to 30 petals. Zones 6 to 9. RIR=7.7

'Salet' (1854); moss. Medium-size bush, 4 to 5 feet tall. Covered with small bloom clusters. Moderately recurrent. Fragrant. Can suffer from mildew if unprotected. 35 to 40 petals. Zones 4 to 10. RIR=8.1

'Sombreuil' (1850); climbing tea. A favorite climber in moderate climates (PSW, SC and ASE), 10 to 12 feet tall. Self-cleaning. 45 to 50 petals. Zones 7 to 9. RIR=8.8

'Souvenir de la Malmaison' (1843); bourbon. Blooms open to flat, quartered masterpieces with spicy fragrance. Hates rain. 4 feet tall. A climbing counterpart is available. 35 to 40 petals. Zones 6 to 9. RIR=8.7

'Superb Tuscan' (pre-1848); gallica. Large, dark blooms with contrasting golden yellow stamens appear once in summer. 4 to 5 feet tall. 35 to 40 petals. Zones 4 to 10. RIR=8.5

'Zephirine Drouhin' (1868); bourbon. Long-flowering climber, 10 to 12 feet tall. Nearly thornless stems. Distinctive fragrance in warm climates. Tolerates shade. 30 to 35 petals. Zones 5 to 10. RIR=8.1

Classic Shrubs

In the case of shrubs, there are four classifications: hybrid rugosa, kordesii, hybrid musk, and shrub. Whatever the classification, varieties belonging to these classes are often characterized as vigorous, large, and generally disease resistant. Known for their ability to grow in the most hostile of environments—both hot and cold—they survive in spite of neglect. But with regular care they can make wonderful landscape possibilities come true. Within this group the diversity of form, color, and habit can be vast—from the simplicity of single-petaled elegance to graceful multipetaled classics reminiscent of their near cousins, the old garden roses.

The hybrid rugosa derived its name from its characteristic deep-furrowed foliage. It is both hardy and disease resistant. Kordesii are large, dense plants ideally suited to landscaping or training as climbers. Hybrid musks are also large, repeat-blooming varieties that can grow up to 20 feet in every direction and are commonly used for trellises and growing up into trees. Shrub is a generic term used to describe varieties with a less formal character. They can have either a sprawling habit and a tendency to grow 15 to 20 feet or more in every direction—or just form a dense, compact, medium-size bush. Noted for hardiness, shrubs are usually quite vigorous and produce large quantities of flower clusters from late spring into fall. These varieties did not fit neatly into the old garden rose scheme and a catch-all classification was employed in an attempt to give them a rightful place in the rose family tree.

However, over the last decade a further subdivision within the shrub classification created by the American Rose Society has emerged. A designation of "classic" describes the hybrid rugosas, kordesiis, and hybrid musks, while the term "modern" is used to describe all other shrubs (see page 82). This section deals with the classic shrub grouping, plus several shrub species distinctly different from the evolution of modern shrub roses, which will be discussed on page 82.

'Ballerina' (1937); hybrid musk. Outstanding landscape plant. Hydrangea-like clusters throughout the season. Vigorous. Disease resistant. Can be trained as a climber reaching 10 feet, or groomed as a neat 5-foot shrub. 5 to 12 petals. Zones 4 to 9. RIR=8.8

'All That Jazz' (1992); shrub; AARS. Blooms in large clusters on an upright bush, 4 to 5 feet tall. Waxy polished foliage impervious to disease. Vigorous growth that just won't quit. 5 to 10 petals. Zones 5 to 9. RIR=7.6

'Blanc Double de Coubert' (1892); hybrid rugosa. Delicate recurrent blooms with very sweet fragrance. Typical wrinkled foliage; 5 to 7 feet tall. Intermittently sets hips in the fall. 20 to 25 petals. Zones 3 to 9. RIR=8.7

'Bonica' (1987); shrub; AARS. Florets in giant clusters; some fragrance. Plant prefers to spread with long, arching canes 3 to 4 feet high rather than grow tall. Ideal for use as a ground cover. Foliage is small and disease free. 40+ petals. Zones 4 to 9. RIR=8.5

'Buff Beauty' (1939); hybrid musk. Reblooming. Fresh scent. 8 to 10 feet tall. 50 petals. Zones 4 to 9. RIR=8.3

'Carefree Beauty' (1977); shrub. Non-stop medium-size clusters. Medium-green foliage. Very disease resistant. Upright, 5 to 6 feet tall. Hardy. 9 to 15 petals. Zones 4 to 9. RIR=8.5

'Carefree Delight' (1996); shrub; AARS. Flowers in small clusters cover 3- to 4-foot mounded plants spring to fall. Vigorous, disease resistant. 5 petals. Zones 4 to 10.

'Carefree Wonder' (1991); shrub; AARS. Large, radiant flowers with a white eye and cream reverse are borne in small clusters. Superb disease resistance, hardiness, and neat growth habit make this a top performer. 20 to 25 petals. Zones 3 to 9. RIR=8.0

'Cornelia' (1919); hybrid musk. Large fragrant flowers all year in flat clusters. Extremely vigorous, 8 to 10 feet tall in warm climates. In the fall the plant provides a display of hips. 20 to 25 petals. Zones 6 to 9. RIR=9.0

'Dortmund' (1955); kordesii. Blooms in medium-size clusters all summer. Vigorous. Grows 10 to 15 feet tall as freestanding shrub or trained as a climber. Fall display of bright orange hips adds winter appeal. Very disease resistant and hardy. 5 to 12 petals. Zones 4 to 9. RIR=9.4

'Erfurt' (1939); hybrid musk. Very fragrant, single-petaled, recurrent flowers. Trailing bushy habit, 6 feet tall. 10 petals. Zones 4 to 9. RIR=8.5

'Felicia' (1928); hybrid musk. Fragrant flowers all summer. Grow as 5-foot-tall pillar or shrub. Disease resistant. 15 to 20 petals. Zones 6 to 9. RIR=8.3

'Frau Dagmar Hartopp' (1914); hybrid rugosa. Fragrant single flowers bloom continuously on 4-foot plants. Foliage is rich green and wrinkled. Large crimson hips in fall. 5 petals. Zones 3 to 9. RIR=8.5

'F.J. Grootendorst' (1918); hybrid rugosa. Florets have serrated edges in clusters of up to 20 spring to fall. Light fragrance. Bushy, 6 feet tall. 15 to 20 petals. Zones 4 to 10. RIR=7.7

'Flutterbye' (1996); shrub. Ever-changing color in large clusters as blooms open on strong stems. Disease resistant. 6 to 7 feet tall; can be trained as climber in warm climates. 5 to 8 petals. Zones 5 to 11

Classic Shrubs
continued

'Gartendirektor Otto Linne' (1934); shrub. 30-bloom clusters all summer. Apple-green leaves. Disease resistant, vigorous, 6 to 10 feet tall. Train as climber in mild climates. 25 petals. Zones 4 to 9. RIR=8.9

'Pink Grootendorst' (1923); hybrid rugosa. Masses of small florets with frilled edges. Wrinkled foliage, 6 feet tall. Makes an excellent hedge. 20 petals or more. Zones 4 to 9. RIR=7.8

'Gruss an Aachen' (1909). Dwarf, compact, 3 to 4 feet high. Abundant, large double flowers age gracefully to creamy white. Fragrant. Foliage is leathery, dark, and disease resistant. 40 to 45 petals. Zones 4 to 9. RIR=8.3

'Hansa' (1905); hybrid rugosa. Clove fragrance, strong stems. Vigorous and very hardy but sensitive to pesticides, 4 to 5 feet tall. Striking hips. 30 petals. Zones 3 to 9. RIR=8.3

'Kaleidoscope' (1999); shrub; AARS. Unusual, pleasing, complementary colors. 3 to 4 feet tall. 35 to 40 petals. Zones 5 to 11.

'Kathleen' (1922); hybrid musk. Single-petaled large clusters spring to fall. Golden stamens. Vigorous, 6 to 12 feet tall. Orange hips in fall. 5 petals. Zones 6 to 9. RIR=8.8

'Lavender Dream' (1984); shrub. Masses of 2- to 3-inch semi-double blossoms all summer. Tends to throw out arching canes 5 feet tall by 5 feet wide. 16 petals. Zones 4 to 9. RIR=8.3

'Lavender Lassie' (1960); hybrid musk. Large trusses of very fragrant flowers. Pillar growth habit, 8 to 12 feet tall. Foliage is disease resistant. 25 to 30 petals. Zones 4 to 9. RIR=8.0

'Linda Campbell' (1990); hybrid rugosa. Tall, arching canes 8 to 10 feet tall. Huge sprays, repeat bloomer. Likes heat (ASE and SC). 20 to 25 petals. Zones 4 to 11. RIR=7.4

'Nymphenburg' (1954); hybrid musk. Abundant, fragrant, large flowers in large clusters. Pillar or upright bush 8 to 10 feet tall. Disease resistant. 20+ petals. Zones 4 to 10. RIR=8.6

'Oranges 'n' Lemons' (1995); shrub. Fantastic color all summer in a fountain of tall, arching canes 8 feet tall by 8 feet wide. Prefers cool climates, such as NC and ANE. 30 to 35 petals. Zones 4 to 10.

'Paul's Himalayan Musk' (1916); rambler. Rosette blooms in large clusters on thread-like stems. Can grow to 30 feet in all directions. Ideal for growing on trees. Zones 4 to 9

'Prosperity' (1919); hybrid musk. Recurrent flowers in large clusters. Vigorous. Train as a tall pillar. Very fragrant. 20 petals. Zones 4 to 9. RIR=8.5

'Queen Margrethe' (1995); shrub. Heavy-quartered blooms. Manageable round compact bush growing 4 to 5 feet tall. Disease free. Lovely apple fragrance. 50 petals or more. Zones 5 to 10.

Rosa rugosa rubra (pre-1799); species. Blooms are best in spring with fat round bright red hips in fall. Quilted foliage, 5 to 6 feet tall. Very hardy. 5 petals. Zones 3 to 10. RIR=9.3

Rosa rugosa alba (pre-1800); species. White form of Rosa rugosa, with the same hardiness, lovely hips, and vigor. 5 petals. Zones 3 to 10. RIR=9.3

'Roserie de l'Hay' (1901); hybrid rugosa. Large loose blooms open perfectly flat; repeat-blooming with a. sugared-almond fragrance. Grows 5 to 6 feet tall. 30+ petals. Zones 4 to 9. RIR=9.0

'Sally Holmes' (1976); shrub. Large, long-lasting clusters cover a large spreading bush, 10 feet tall and wide. First spring bloom is best. Needs lots of space. Makes good pillar. 5 to 8 petals. Zones 4 to 9. RIR=8.9

'Sunny June' (1952); shrub. Single-petaled, repeated blooms cover polished, dark green leaves. Can stand alone or be trained on a trellis, 8 feet tall. Vigorous. 5 to 7 petals. Zones 5 to 10. RIR=7.7

'Therese Bugnet' (1950); hybrid rugosa. Flowers over dark green foliage. Remarkably disease resistant. Can suffer badly from chemical sprays. 4 to 6 feet tall. 35 to 40 petals. Zones 3 to 10. RIR=8.1

'Topaz Jewel' (1987); hybrid rugosa. Rare recurrent-blooming yellow rugosa. Fragrant. Disease resistant, hardy, vigorous, 4 to 6 feet tall. 25+ petals. Zones 6 to 9. RIR=7.3

'William Baffin' (1983). Ovoid buds open to double flowers in giant clusters of 30 flowers or more. Foliage is fairly disease resistant. Plant tends to climb with spreading growth, 5 to 6 feet high. 20 petals. Zones 3 to 9. RIR=9.4

Modern Shrubs

In the early 1970s, a new group of modern shrub roses became popular. This additional division was deemed necessary to recognize the evolutionary work of David Austin in England. By crossing old garden roses with modern roses such as hybrid teas and floribundas, Austin gave birth to a new type of modern shrub rose (he calls them English roses). These were marked by the fragrances and romantic flower forms of old garden roses, but with the recurrent blooming, vigor, hardiness, and color range of modern hybrids.

Other breeders have contributed to this modern shrub group, such as the hardy shrubs of Dr. Griffith Buck from Iowa, ground covers from Kordes in Germany, Romantica roses from Meilland in France, Generosa roses from Guillot in France, Country Roses from Harkness in England, and some Moore roses from California. Like Austin's roses, these were developed by crossing old garden roses with modern roses, retaining the best features of both. The return of old-fashioned fragrances such as myrrh, citrus, apple, damask, and musk enhances their appeal. Many modern shrub roses are root hardy in zones 4 to 10, but perform best with winter protection in zone 6 and further north.

'Abbaye de Cluny' (1996). Austin. Antique rose-shaped blooms are vibrant and fragrant. Repeat flowering is fast on this European award winner. Vigorous; 3 to 4 feet tall. 30 petals. Zones 4 to 9.

'Charles Rennie Mackintosh' (1988). Austin. Cupped flowers. Vigorous and very thorny bush. Remove spent blooms to promote next cycle. 4 to 6 feet tall. Powerful fragrance. 50 petals. Zones 4 to 9.

'Claudia Cardinale' (1997). Guillot. One of the new Generosa roses from France with quartered, egg-yolk-yellow blooms that age to copper-red. Grows 5 to 6 feet tall. 40 to 50 petals. Zones 5 to 10.

'Colette' (1998). Meilland. Strong climber covers itself and landscape with blooms in small sprays. The French breeder calls the variety a 'Romantica Rose'. 10 to 12 feet tall. Damask fragrance. 25 petals. Zones 4 to 9.

'Constance Spry' (1961). Austin's first introduction. One bloom cycle in the spring. Will sprawl 10 to 12 feet in all directions. Strong myrrh fragrance. 50 petals. Zones 4 to 9. RIR=8.5

'Country Dancer' (1973). Buck. A dwarf shrub, 3 to 4 feet tall with large double blooms in clusters on dark green foliage. Light fragrance. Vigorous. Zones 4 to 9. RIR=8.4

'Country Fair' (1996). Harkness. Very large sprays of delicate blooms (40 to 50 per stem) mature to a lighter color with golden stamens. Well-rounded, medium-size bush, 4 to 6 feet tall. 25 to 30 petals. Zones 4 to 9.

'Country Lady' (1987). Harkness. Blooms color in reverse and change with age, one to a stem or in small clusters. Spicy fragrance. 4 to 6 feet tall. 35 to 40 petals. Zones 4 to 9.

'Country Life' (1996). Harkness. Large fragrant blooms on small clusters repeat well in most climates. Grows like a floribunda. Good vigor and hardiness. 4 to 6 feet tall. 30 to 35 petals. Zones 4 to 9.

'Country Music' (1996). Harkness. Large clusters of sensuous blooms on strong, straight, nearly thornless stems hold their color even in hot sun. Low, vigorous shrub, 4 to 6 feet tall. 25 to 30 petals. Zones 4 to 9.

'Eden' (1987). Meilland. Also known as 'Pierre de Ronsard'. Climber from French Romantica collection. Blooms in small clusters on vigorous disease-resistant bush. Ideal for lampposts and gazebos. 10 to 12 feet tall. Lightly fragrant. 40+ petals. Zones 4 to 9.

'Earth Song' (1975). Buck. Long urn-shaped buds open to large flowers with strong fragrance. Grandiflora-like habit, 4 to 6 feet tall. 25 petals. Zones 3 to 9. RIR=8.1

Modern Shrubs
continued

'Evelyn' (1991). Austin. Shallow-cupped blooms in shades of apricot-yellow. 4 to 5 feet. 50+ petals. Zones 5 to 10. RIR=7.6.

'Fair Bianca' (1982). Austin. Myrrh-scented symmetrical blossoms. 4 to 5 feet tall. 50+ petals. Zones 4 to 10. RIR=7.9.

'Francois Rabelais' (2000). Meilland. A floribunda with old-fashioned appeal. 3 to 6 feet tall. 25 to 30 petals. Zones 4 to 9.

'Gertrude Jekyll' (1986). Austin. Wonderfully flat blooms with myrrh fragrance. Canes are very thorny. In moderate climates can grow as tall as 10 feet. 50+ petals. Zones 5 to 10.

'Glamis Castle' (1992). Austin. The finest white English rose with a wonderful myrrh fragrance. Florets are cupped and appear through the season. Compact, 3 to 4 feet tall. 50+ petals. Zones 5 to 10.

'Golden Celebration' (1992). Austin. Blooms up to 5 inches across in clusters on strong, straight stems. Rounded, compact, and medium-size, 5 to 6 feet tall. 50+ petals. Zones 4 to 9.

'Graham Thomas' (1983). Austin. Deeply cupped florets. Gains height and density in warm climates, prefers PSW. 6 to 8 feet tall. 50+ petals. Zones 4 to 9. RIR=8.4

'Guy de Maupassant' (1996). Meilland. A Romantica Rose with perfect old-fashioned quartered blooms. Very vigorous. Registered as a floribunda, grows 4 to 6 feet tall. Great fragrance. 90 to 100 petals. Zones 4 to 9.

'Jean Giono' (1996). Meilland. A Romantica Rose, with fragrant flowers on plant with a grandiflora-like habit, 4 to 5 feet tall. Disease resistant, vigorous. 100 petals. Zones 4 to 9.

'Johann Strauss' (1996). Meilland. A Romantica Rose. Sprays of 3 to 7 flowers. Disease resistant. Prolific bloom production. 4 to 5 feet tall. Lemon-verbena fragrance. 100 petals. Zones 4 to 10.

'L.D. Braithwaite' (1988). Austin. Wide, slightly cupped flowers continuously all summer. Dark green, disease-resistant foliage. 4 to 6 feet tall. 50+ petals. Zones 4 to 9.

'Leonardo da Vinci' (1998). Meilland. A Romantica Rose. Weatherproof, sweetly-perfumed blooms in small clusters surrounded by disease-resistant foliage. Plant is vigorous. Grows much like a floribunda, 3 feet tall. 25 to 30 petals. Zones 4 to 9.

'Martine Guillot' (1997). Guillot. A Generosa Rose. Unique shrub with sprays of creamy buds that open to soft apricot. Fresh gardenia scent. Grows 5 to 6 feet tall. 40 to 50 petals. Zones 5 to 10.

'Mary Rose' (1983). Austin. Damask-like flowers with ruffled center petals. Vigorous, disease resistant, 4 to 5 feet tall. 50+ petals. Zones 4 to 11. RIR=8.6

'Molineux' (1994). Austin. Delicately colored repeating rosettes with heavy tea-rose scent. Bushy, upright habit is ideal for a small garden. 3½ feet tall. 50 to 60 petals. Zones 5 to 11.

'Moore's Classic Perpetual' (1998). Moore. Large blossoms on small bush only 2 to 3 feet tall. 50 to 60 petals. Zones 4 to 11.

'Moore's Pink Perpetual' (1997). Moore. Dwarf hybrid repeat bloomer with strongly fragrant large flowers in loose sprays throughout the summer. Makes a great dwarf hedge. Grows 3 feet tall. 40 to 50 petals. Zones 5 to 10.

'Othello' (1986). Austin. Color varies with climate. Use as a large shrub or a low climber, 6 to 7 feet tall. Needs protection from mildew. 50+ petals. Zones 4 to 11. RIR=7.1

Modern Shrubs
continued

'Out of Yesteryear' (1997). Moore. Quartered flowers bloom in clusters non-stop. Disease resistant, grows 4 to 5 feet tall with spreading habit. 40 to 60 petals. Zones 4 to 9.

'Perdita' (1983). Austin. Blooms change from hybrid tea form to quartered cups and finish as neat rosettes. Needs a season to establish. 4 feet tall. 50+ petals. Zones 4 to 9. RIR=7.8

'Polka' (1997). Meilland. A Romantica rose. Repeat-blooming, old-garden-rose flowers. Grows like a climber, 10 to 12 feet tall. Disease resistant. 40 to 50 petals. Zones 4 to 9

'Radio Times' (1994). Austin. Rich rosettes age gracefully with the petals recurving back. Strong fragrance and short, bushy growth only 3 feet tall. 60+ petals. Zones 4 to 9.

'Redoute' (1992). Austin. Sport of 'Mary Rose' with all its characteristics except color. Good repeat flowering, light fragrance. Medium-size bush, 4 feet tall. 40 to 50 petals. Zones 4 to 9.

'Scepter'd Isle' (1996). Austin. The large double blooms have a wonderful scent, good repeat cycle. Shrubby grower, 3 to 4 feet tall. Good disease resistance. Ideal as a border plant. 35 to 40 petals. Zones 4 to 9.

'Sharifa Asma' (1989). Austin. Shallow, gently cupped blooms age to perfectly formed rosettes with good fragrance. Plant is a low grower, 3 feet tall. 40 to 50 petals. Zones 4 to 10.

'Sir Edward Elgar' (1992). Austin. Blooms open to three-dimensional pompons too heavy for stems to hold upright. 4 to 5 feet tall. 50+ petals. Zones 5 to 10.

'Sonia Rykiel' (1995). Guillot. A Generosa Rose. Fragrant, quartered blooms, mostly one per stem. 5 to 6 feet. 40 to 50 petals. Zones 5 to 11.

'Sweet Juliet' (1989). Austin. Lightly cupped, repeat flowering blooms. Vigorous, upright, but graceful plants of medium size, 4 feet tall. 50 to 100 petals. Zones 5 to 10.

'Tamora' (1987). Austin. Deeply cupped, long-repeating blooms have a strong myrrh fragrance. Very thorny. Dense, compact, 3 to 4 feet. 40 to 50 petals. Zones 4 to 9.

'The Pilgrim' (1991). Austin. Fragrant flowers are strong and well shaped, age until outer rows are near-white. Grows to medium height, 3½ feet tall. 50 to 100 petals. Zones 4 to 9.

'The Prince' (1990). Austin. Bloom colors deepen with age. Low-growing, spreading bush, 3 feet tall. Substantial fragrance. 100 petals. Zones 4 to 9.

'Toulouse Lautrec' (1996). Meilland. A Romantica Rose. Clear-colored fragrant blooms. Deep glossy-green foliage on a 5-foot-tall bush. 90 petals. Zones 4 to 9.

'Traviata' (1996). Meilland. A Romantica Rose. Deeply colored quartered blooms with 100 petals, complete with a light fragrance. Vigorous and disease resistant. 4 to 5 feet tall. 100 petals. Zones 4 to 9.

'Yves Piaget' (1989). Meilland. A Romantica Rose. This award-winning variety boasts peony-shaped, mauve-pink blossoms on a hybrid-tea-like plant. Vigorous, dense, upright, 4 feet tall. Hardy and disease free. 50+ petals. Zones 4 to 10. RIR=7.5

Climbers, Ground Covers, and Hedges

A large group of roses is dominated by a predisposition to climb—with long, arching canes that can be trained up fences, over walls, through trellises, arbors, and pergolas. This group of climbers encompasses all flower sizes and shapes, from miniature florets to large hybrid-tea-type blossoms. Within the group there are two subdivisions. The first includes the climbing counterparts of already existing varieties. For example, after the introduction of the hybrid tea 'Double Delight' in 1977, a climbing sport (or mutation) dubbed 'Climbing Double Delight' was introduced in 1982. The flowers are the same, but one is a bush, the other a climber. On page 90 you'll find a list of climbers that appear under other group headings. The second group (discussed here) includes true climbers with no bush rose counterparts.

Page 91 highlights ground cover and hedge roses because of their difference in habit from the traditional bush types. Ground covers boast a low-growing habit that spreads over large areas. Hedge roses have the ability to form a compact hedge if planted close together, about 12 to 18 inches apart.

'Altissimo' (1966); climber. Very large blossoms with golden stamens that spill their pollen onto the petals. Hardy and vigorous, 8 to 10 feet tall. 5 to 7 petals. Zones 6 to 9. RIR=9.5

'America' (1976); climber. AARS. Blooms are perfectly formed; strong spicy fragrance. Late bloomer but repeats well all year. Grows 10 to 12 feet tall. 40 to 45 petals. Zones 6 to 10. RIR=8.5

'Autumn Sunset' (1988); climber. Great hardiness and super disease resistance. Performs best in cool climates, such as PNW and ANE. 8 to 12 feet tall. 20 to 25 petals. Zones 6 to 10. RIR=7.5

'Berries 'n' Cream' (1998); climber. Covered with large clusters on strong stems. Disease-free shrub that blooms all year. Vigorous bush arching 10 to 12 feet high and wide. 25 to 30 petals. Zones 5 to 10.

*'Blaze Improved'
(1932); climber.
Great display of
large clusters.
Consistent
performer with
good repeat
bloom cycle.
12 to 14 feet tall.
20 to 25 petals.
Zones 5 to 10.
RIR=9.1*

*'Don Juan' (1958); climber. Magnificent clusters
of shapely blooms throughout the summer.
Foliage is glossy and dark green on a vigorous
disease-resistant plant. 10 to 12 feet tall. 30 to
35 petals. Zones 6 to 9. RIR=8.2*

*'Dr. J.H.
Nicholas' (1940).
An abundance of
globular,
fragrant blooms,
singly and in
clusters, makes
this an excellent
pillar rose.
Usually grows to
about 8 feet tall
in moderate
climates. 50
petals. Zones 5
to 11. RIR=7.4*

*'Dublin Bay'
(1975); climber.
Lots of blooms
in small sprays.
Train as pillar or
climber. Well-
suited to both
cool climates,
ANE, and
warmer
climates, ASE.
8 to 10 feet tall.
25 petals. Zones
4 to 11. RIR=8.5*

*'Golden Showers'
(1957); climber;
AARS. Small
clusters on a
vigorous bush with
good color finish.
Licorice fragrance.
Best in cool
climates, such as
PNW and ANE.
10 to 12 feet tall. 25
to 28 petals. Zones
6 to 9. RIR=7.4*

*'Joseph's Coat'
(1964); climber.
Popular variety
because of the
multi-toned
color display.
Produces lots of
big clusters
throughout the
growing season.
10 to 12 feet tall.
23 to 28 petals.
Zones 4 to 10.
RIR=7.5*

*'Handel' (1965); climber. Blooms generally come one to a
stem or in small sprays. Best in cool climates, such as
ANE and PNW. 10 to 12 feet tall. 20 to 30 petals. Zones 5
to 9. RIR=8.2*

Climbers
continued

'Fourth of July' (1999); climber; AARS. Super-vigorous climber provides big sprays of long-lasting striped blooms with apple-and-rose fragrance. Grows 10 to 14 feet tall. 10 to 15 petals. Zones 5 to 11.

'Mlle Cecile Brunner' (1894); climbing polyantha. Large sprays cover the plant. Grows 20 to 30 feet in all directions; can cover a house or climb a tree. 30+ petals. Zones 6 to 10. RIR=8.3

'New Dawn' (1930); climber; elected to the Rose Hall of Fame. Fragrant flowers appear all season. Extremely vigorous and hardy. Grows well in nearly all climates. 18 to 20 feet tall. 35 to 40 petals. Zones 4 to 10. RIR=8.5

'Royal Sunset' (1960); climber. Blooms are large, set against deep, glossy, dark green foliage and appear in abundance all summer. Vigorous. Best in cool climates, such as PWN and ANE. 8 to 10 feet tall. Moderate fragrance. 20 to 25 petals. Zones 6 to 10. RIR=9.2

OTHER CLIMBERS

In other sections of this selection guide (especially in the hybrid tea, floribunda, and miniature rose sections), you will find roses that have climbing versions. These varieties are usually sports or mutations that resemble the original in flower form and color but often are less hardy and bear fewer blooms. The most popular of these climbing varieties are:

HYBRID TEAS: 'Climbing Double Delight', 'Climbing First Prize', 'Climbing Paradise', 'Climbing Queen Elizabeth', and 'Climbing Peace'.

MINIATURES: 'Climbing Rainbow's End' and 'Climbing Mary Marshall'.

POLYANTHAS: 'Climbing Cecile Brunner'.

FLORIBUNDAS: 'Climbing Angel Face', 'Climbing Circus', 'Climbing Iceberg', 'Climbing Playgirl', 'Climbing Sunsprite', and 'Climbing Sun Flare'.

OLD GARDEN ROSES: 'Climbing Souvenir de la Malmaison', 'Climbing Mrs. B.R. Cant', and 'Climbing Old Blush China'.

Additionally, some roses in other sections have growth habits with long, arching canes that allow them to be trained as climbers. They include:

MINIATURES: 'Jeanne LaJoie'.

OLD GARDEN ROSES: 'Austrian Copper', 'Celine Forestier', 'Madame Alfred Carriere', 'Madame Isaac Pereire', 'Marechal Niel', 'Mermaid', 'Reine des Violettes', 'Rev d'Or', 'Sombreuil', and 'Zephirine Drouhin'.

CLASSIC SHRUBS: 'Ballerina', 'Dortmund', 'Lavender Lassie', 'Sally Holmes', and 'Oranges and Lemons'.

MODERN SHRUBS: 'Colette', 'Constance Spry', 'Eden', and 'Polka'.

'White Dawn' (1949); climber. Proven performer displays weatherproof ruffled blooms spring to fall. Vigorous and disease free, 10 to 12 feet tall. Performs well in all climates. 30 to 35 petals. Zones 6 to 9. RIR=7.7

Ground Covers and Hedges

'Flower Carpet' (1989). Ground cover with exemplary vigor and disease resistance. Massive clusters on strong arching stems. Grows 24 to 32 inches tall; 4 feet wide. Other colors are now available in this series. 5 to 20 petals. Zones 4 to 11.

'Nearly Wild' (1941). Covered in spring with single flowers. Attractive foliage. Best in mass plantings. Hardy. Zones 4 to 10. RIR=7.4

Fuchsia Meidiland

Meidiland Landscape Roses. Wonderful series of low maintenance roses. Pest resistant, disease tolerant, hardy. Non-stop, long-lasting, brilliant blooms. Landscape opportunities range from hedges to ground cover. White ground covers include 'Alba Meidiland', 'Ice Meidiland', and 'White Meidiland'; in red there is 'Magic Meidiland' 'Sevillana' and 'Red Meidiland'. Pink hedge roses include 'Bonica', 'Royal Bonica', and 'Pink Meidiland'; in reds, 'Cherry Meidiland' and 'Coral Meidiland'. White Meidiland RIR=8.2; Alba Meidiland RIR=8.3; Red Meidiland RIR=7.1; Pink Meidiland RIR=8.6. Zones 5 to 10.

Pearl Meidiland

Red Meidiland

'Red Ribbons' (1996). Long-lasting flowers on vigorous plants 6 feet wide, 2 feet tall. Zones 4 to 11.

Yellow Simplicity

Pink Simplicity

Red Simplicity

'Simplicity' (1978); floribunda. Hardy and disease-resistant rose for hedges, 4-5 feet tall. Everblooming. Plant 2 feet apart to form a dense hedge. 18 petals. This is a series that comes in a variety of colors. Zones 4 to 11. RIR=8.0

White Simplicity

GOOD GROUND COVERS FROM OTHER SECTIONS

MINIATURES:
'Gourmet Popcorn' and 'Green Ice'.
SHRUBS:
'Bonica' and 'Country Music'.

GOOD HEDGES FROM OTHER SECTIONS

FLORIBUNDAS:
'Iceberg' and 'The Fairy'.
SHRUBS:
'Ballerina', 'Carefree Delight', 'Country Fair', and 'Moore's Pink Perpetual'.

How to Find Out More About Roses

Gardeners who enjoy growing roses often need help and assistance as well as want to share their experiences. The American Rose Society (ARS) is a national nonprofit organization composed of a network of about 400 local rose societies in cities and towns throughout the United States. Headquartered in Shreveport, Louisiana, the ARS maintains a 118-acre park known as the American Rose Center, which is dedicated to roses. With more than 22,000 members, the ARS offers many services to promote rose-growing:

■ Provides access to more than 2,800 experts who offer personal rose growing assistance. There's one in your area who can help answer your questions and recommend solutions to your problems.

■ Lists affiliated rose societies in your area where you can learn even more about rose growing and make new friends.

■ Publishes an annual *Handbook for Selecting Roses*, which ranks and rates new roses.

■ Publishes a 42-page, full-color monthly magazine, *The American Rose*, devoted to cultural information, tips, and advice.

■ Publishes the *American Rose Annual*, a 160-page, full-color volume containing the latest information on roses and rose culture.

■ Publishes four quarterly publications dealing with specialized subjects: *Miniature Roses, Old Garden Roses, Rose Arrangements*, and *Rose Exhibiting*.

■ Maintains a lending library of books, videos, and slide series that can be borrowed through the mail.

■ Holds annual national conventions and rose shows each year featuring lectures, garden tours, and a chance to meet with fellow rose growers from all over the nation.

Joining the ARS is certainly a step to becoming a better rose grower. The benefits of membership can lead you to expanding your garden, gaining new friendships, and, most of all, improving your rose-growing techniques. For more information, call 800-637-6534 or write to: American Rose Society, P.O. Box 30,000, Shreveport, LA 71130-0300.

EXPLORING THE INTERNET FOR ROSE INFORMATION

The following rose societies and organizations have web pages crammed full of color photos, and information on new roses and rose growing:

■ **All-America Rose Selection** (www.rose.org) provides lists and photographs of all previous award winners from 1940 to the present. The website also has a search feature that allows visitors to access a list of prominent rose gardens by state.

■ **American Rose Society** (www.ars.org) offers features such as "Rose of the Month," articles by experts on selected topics, links to local rose societies, answers to frequently asked questions, where to buy roses, and much more. This site is updated regularly with news and events and deserves frequent visits. It also includes various links to associated websites.

■ **Canadian Rose Society** (www.mirror.org/groups/crs) lists current events and shows, public gardens, instructions on how to plant roses, explorer roses.

■ **World Federation of Rose Societies** (www.worldrose.org) provides a global perspective on roses, plus the Rose Hall of Fame, listing varieties that have been voted as deserving of the title. Site lists "Coming Events" with worldwide conferences and conventions, and editorials from their newsletter, *World Rose News*. Also includes links to national rose societies.

■ **Royal National Rose Society** (www.roses.co.uk) offers the benefits of membership plus an insight into rose gardens in the United Kingdom, rose care information, events, publications, and more.

INDEX

Page numbers in italics denote photographs.

MAJOR MAIL ORDER SOURCES

Requested catalogs via mail or telephone.

MAINLY LARGE ROSES
Arena Rose Company, P.O. Box 3096, Paso Robles, California 93447.
  Tel: (805) 227-4094
Edmunds Roses, 6235 SW Kahla Road, Wilsonville, Oregon 97070.
  Tel: (503) 682-1476
Jackson & Perkins, 1 Rose Lane, Medford, Oregon 97501.
  Tel: (800) 292-4769
Spring Hill Nurseries, 110 West Elm Street, Tipp City, Ohio 45371.
  Tel: (800) 582-8527
Wayside Gardens, 1 Garden Lane, Hodges, South Carolina 29695.
  Tel: (800) 845-1124

MINIATURE ROSES
Bridges Roses, 2734 Toney Road, Lawndale, North Carolina 28090.
  Tel: (704) 538-9412
Nor'East Miniature Roses, 58 Hammond Street, Rowley, Massachusettes
  01969. Tel: (800) 426-6485
Sequoia Nursery, Moore Miniature Roses, 2519 East Noble Avenue,
  Visalia, California 93292. Tel:(209) 732-0190
Taylor's Roses, P.O. Box 677, Fairhope, Alabama 36533 Tel: (334) 928-5008.
The Mini Rose Garden, Box 203, Austin Street, Cross Hill, South Carolina
  29332. Tel: (864)998-4331

OLD GARDEN ROSES
The Antique Rose Emporium, Route 5, Box 143, Brenham, Texas 77833.
  Tel: (800) 441-0002
Heirloom Old Garden Roses, 24062 Riverside Drive NE, St. Paul, Oregon
  97137. Tel: (503) 538-1576.
Pickering Nurseries, Inc., 670 Kingston Road, Pickering, Ontario L1V
  1A6, Canada. Tel: (905) 839-2111

HARDY OWN-ROOT ROSES
Corn Hill Nursery, Ltd., R.R. 5, Petitcodiac, N.B., EOA 2HO, Canada.
  Tel: (506) 756-3635.

METRIC CONVERSIONS

U.S. Units to Metric Equivalents			Metric Units to U.S. Equivalents		
To Convert From	Multiply By	To Get	To Convert From	Multiply By	To Get
Inches	25.4	Millimeters	Millimeters	0.0394	Inches
Inches	2.54	Centimeters	Centimeters	0.3937	Inches
Feet	30.48	Centimeters	Centimeters	0.0328	Feet
Feet	0.3048	Meters	Meters	3.2808	Feet
Yards	0.9144	Meters	Meters	1.0936	Yards
Cubic feet	0.0283	Cubic meters	Cubic meters	35.315	Cubic feet
Cubic feet	28.316	Liters	Liters	0.0353	Cubic feet
Cubic yards	0.7646	Cubic meters	Cubic meters	1.308	Cubic yards
Cubic yards	764.55	Liters	Liters	0.0013	Cubic yards

To convert from degrees Fahrenheit (F) to degrees Celsius (C), first subtract 32, then multiply by 5/9.

To convert from degrees Celsius to degrees Fahrenheit, multiply by 9/5, then add 32.